Journeys for Freedom

A New Look at America's Story

Susan Buckley and Elspeth Leacock

Illustrations by Rodica Prato

Houghton Mifflin Company
Boston 2006

The text of this book is set in Palatino.
Book design by Kevin Ullrich

Library of Congress Cataloging-in-Publication Data

Buckley, Susan.
  Journeys for freedom : a new look at America's story / Susan Buckley and Elspeth
Leacock ; illustrations by Rodica Prato.
    p. cm.
  ISBN 0-618-22323-1
  1. United States—History—Anecdotes—Juvenile literature. 2. United States—
Biography—Anecdotes—Juvenile literature. 3. Liberty—History—Anecdotes—Juvenile
literature. 4. United States—History—Maps for children. I. Leacock, Elspeth. II. Prato,
Rodica. III. Title.
  E178.3.B924 2005
  973—dc22   2004000974

ISBN-13: 978-0618-22323-7

Manufactured in China
SCP 10 9 8 7 6 5 4 3 2 1

*For our families and for all who work for freedom—
may they have the world they so deserve.*

*And for Isi, who has kept his love of life
despite everything.*

—S.B., E.L., and R.P.

Note to the Reader

You will notice both double and single quotation marks in this book. We
use double quotation marks when we know exactly what someone said.
We use single quotation marks when we have invented statements
based on historical evidence.

Introduction

Pilgrims and pioneers, immigrants and refugees, soldiers and farmers—Americans all, we have been on a journey for freedom since the beginning of our history. It's a complicated, complex story, but freedom has always been at its heart: what freedom is and why we care so much about it, who has freedom and who does not, who gives freedom and who takes it away, how to get freedom and how to keep it.

An African American couple travels north, risking death. A ten-year-old boy walks 2,000 miles to find a place to worship freely. A Chinese man works thousands of miles away from his beloved family. A Nez Perce woman flees her homeland, pursued by soldiers. What led these people to make such dangerous journeys? What is it about freedom that drives ordinary people to do such extraordinary things?

The twenty stories in *Journeys for Freedom* are true stories, every one of them. The struggles, the losses, and the triumphs of Roger Williams and Teedyuscung and Free Frank and Wetatonmi and Isi Veleris and Lynda Blackmon and Nien Cheng and all of the others are the story of the United States. It is your story too, for all of these journeys for freedom have made the United States what it is today.

Gaining freedom and keeping freedom take great courage and hard work. For ourselves and for our nation, it is a journey that is never finished.

Contents

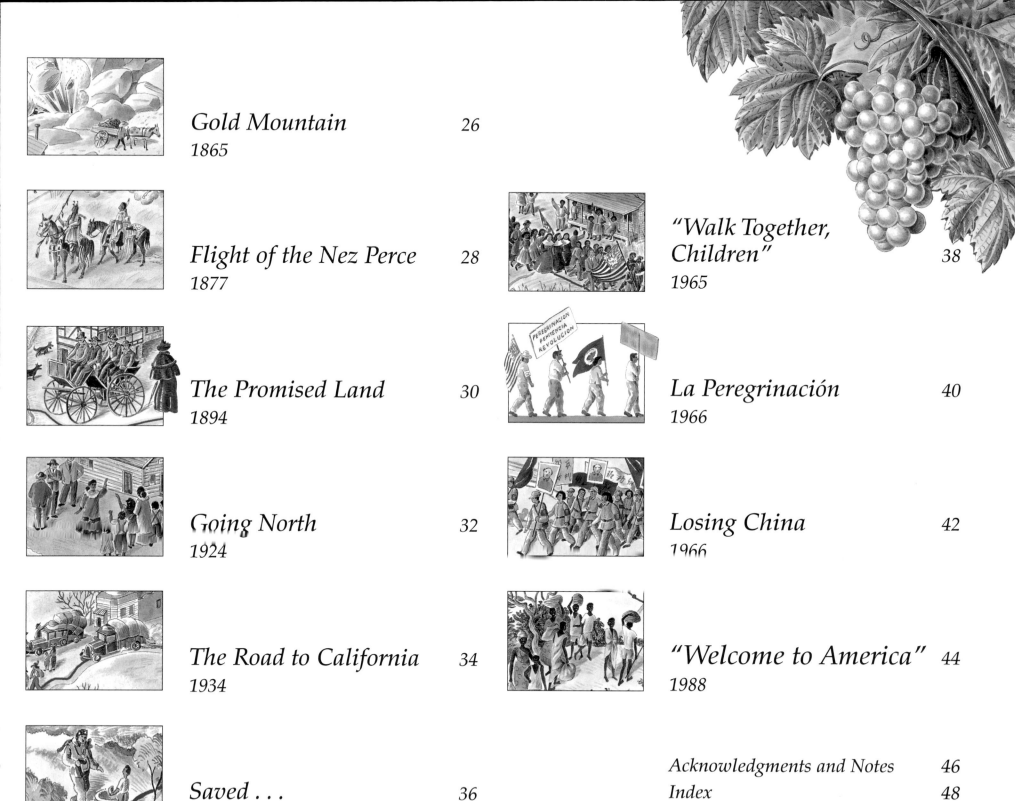

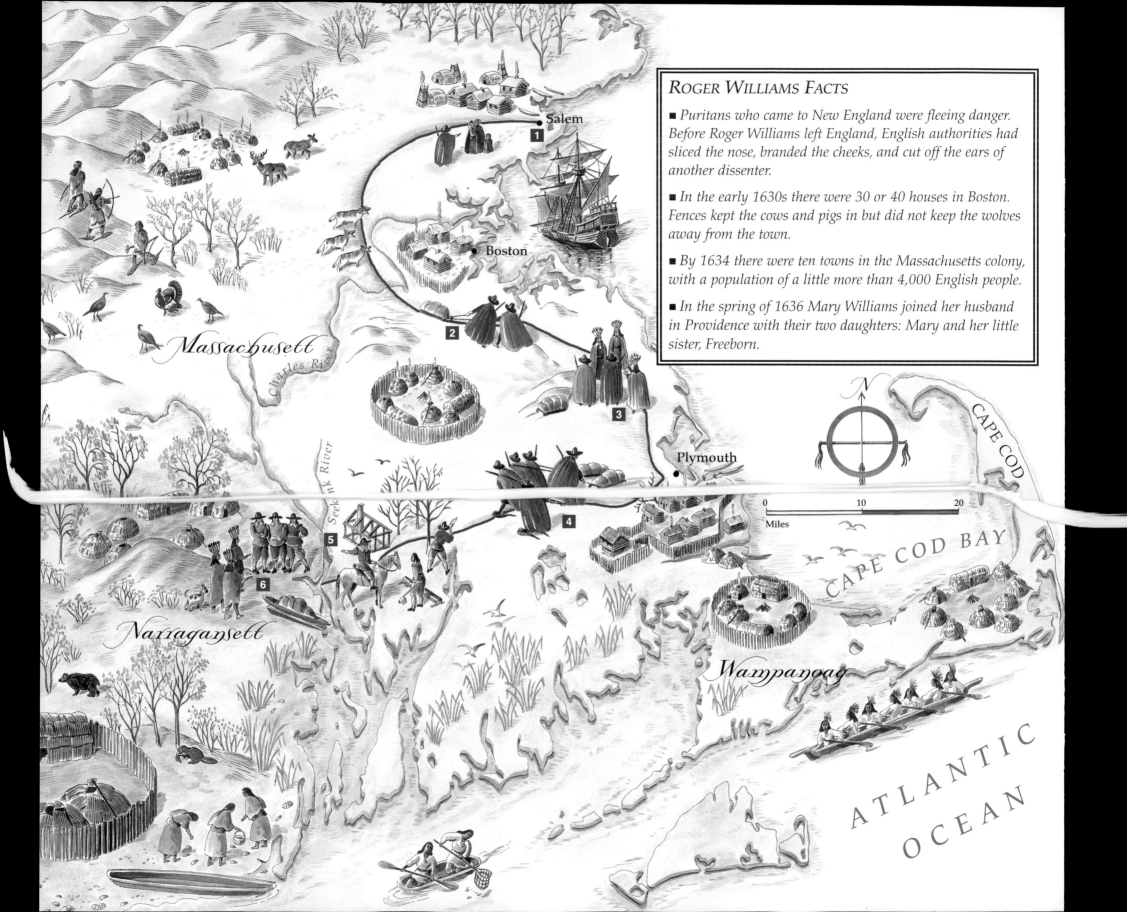

Roger Williams Facts

■ Puritans who came to New England were fleeing danger. Before Roger Williams left England, English authorities had sliced the nose, branded the cheeks, and cut off the ears of another dissenter.

■ In the early 1630s there were 30 or 40 houses in Boston. Fences kept the cows and pigs in but did not keep the wolves away from the town.

■ By 1634 there were ten towns in the Massachusetts colony, with a population of a little more than 4,000 English people.

■ In the spring of 1636 Mary Williams joined her husband in Providence with their two daughters: Mary and her little sister, Freeborn.

Salem

Boston

Massachusett

Charles River

Seekonk River

Plymouth

N

CAPE COD

0   10   20
Miles

CAPE COD BAY

Narragansett

Wampanoag

ATLANTIC OCEAN

To Providence

1631

Roger and Mary Williams stared out at the cold New England shore as the *Lyon* sailed past the ice into Boston Harbor. For 57 days the ship had tossed its way from England to America on the rough winter seas of the North Atlantic. Now the 20 passengers welcomed the sight of the tiny English settlement. The families of Boston welcomed the *Lyon*'s 200 tons of food and supplies. Many settlers had already died in the bitter Massachusetts winter.

Roger Williams, a 27-year-old minister, had come to stay. Back in England, people had called him "divinely mad," because whatever Roger Williams believed in, he believed it strongly. His beliefs led him to leave England, and to separate from the Church of England. Soon he would leave Boston too. 'You must separate completely from the Church of England,' Williams demanded of the Boston Puritans. Angry and insulted, they refused.

In nearby Salem there were more Separatists, people who believed as Roger Williams did. But when they called Williams to preach at their church, powerful Bostonians disapproved. Soon the young minister and his wife moved to Plymouth. For two years they made a life with the 300 Pilgrims settled along the rocky coast.

Roger Williams met the Wampanoag and other native people who lived near Plymouth. This land was the Indians' home, and they came in and out of the English settlements all the time. Williams traded with them, made friends with them, and began to learn their languages. As usual, Roger Williams looked at things a little differently from the way others did. 'The land belongs to the Indians, and it is a sin to seize it,' he said. So Williams made treaties with Canonicus and other Indian leaders for the right to settle on their land.

Pretty soon, the opinionated young minister found himself in trouble again. In 1634, the Salem church asked Roger Williams to come back.

Once there, though, he did not keep quiet. He protested taking Indian land. He protested ties to the Church of England. And he protested the government's right to make rules about religious matters. Church and state must be separate, he challenged.

Finally, the leaders in Boston had had enough. In 1635 the General Court ordered Roger Williams to renounce his views. When he refused, the court banished Williams from Massachusetts because of his "dangerous opinions."

Williams knew he had to flee. By now it was January, in a terrible winter of deep snow and howling winds. Williams said farewell to his family **1** and slipped away with a young servant, Thomas Angell. His best hope, he knew, was to head south **2** to his friends, the Wampanoag and the Narragansett. He planned to build a small settlement for his family and a few supporters, on land he had purchased earlier.

Stopping along the way, the men were welcomed in Indian settlements. **3** Soon they were joined by a few companions from Salem, carrying the tools they would need to start their new lives. **4** Reaching a cove along the banks of the Seekonk River, the men waited for spring. When the weather was warm enough, they began to plant and build. **5** Then bad news arrived. A messenger came to say that Williams had settled on land claimed by Plymouth.

On an April day in 1636 Roger Williams set out to find yet another home. Knowing he would be welcomed, he paddled a canoe down the Seekonk toward a Narragansett settlement. Near where the river flowed into the bay, Williams found a "sweet spring" and fertile land. **6** Buying the right to settle land from the Narragansett, he called the place Providence because he had "a sense of God's merciful providence" in his time of distress. Roger Williams had followed his conscience. He had come at last to a place where he could be free to believe as he believed and to allow others to do the same.

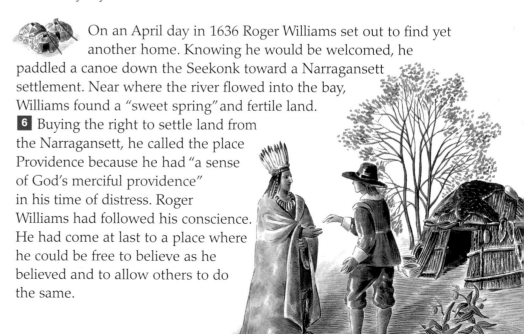

Canonicus   Roger Williams

Le Grand Dérangement

1755

Flames from the burning fields lit the September sky around Grand Pré. **1** Terrified and angry, Elizabeth Brasseux comforted her crying children, Marguerite, Marie-Madeleine, and little Pierre. She longed for her husband, Cosme, and her older sons, Charles and Joseph. The more than 400 men and teenaged boys of Grand Pré had been locked away in the church **2** by British soldiers, who feared the Acadians' fierce protection of their loved ones and their land. Now one of the hated soldiers commanded Elizabeth Brasseux to pack what she could fit into a tiny trunk. **3** 'That's all you can take with you, that and the clothes on your back,' he snarled.

For weeks, the Acadians of Grand Pré had fought against this moment. Rumors had spread through the countryside that the British, who now controlled Nova Scotia, would force them to leave their homeland. Acadians like the Brasseux family had come to Nova Scotia from France 150 years earlier. They had settled the land and built

LOUISIANA

Mississippi River

APPALACHIAN MOUNTAINS

Baltimore **6**

5

Thirteen Colonies

ATLANTIC OCEAN

9 **8**
St. Gabriel · New Orleans

7

GULF OF MEXICO

earn. When her husband died, Elizabeth Brasseux was forced to beg from house to house. **6** As her children grew up in this strange and hostile world, Elizabeth taught them always to remember their past, their language, their faith.

In 1767 word came that Acadians were welcome in the former French colony of Louisiana. Perhaps there, some Acadians thought, they could rebuild their lives. As the head of her family, Elizabeth Brasseux asked the government of Maryland for aid in "removing to the French Settlements on the River Mississippi." With more than 200 other Acadians from Maryland, the Brasseux family sailed on the ship *Jane* on March 2, 1767. **7** Four months later, they arrived in Louisiana. **8**

In the steamy hot days of July, the Acadians petitioned the Louisiana governor for land where they could settle at last. Governor Antonio de Ulloa knew where he wanted to send these brave and hard-working souls: along the Mississippi River to protect the borders of his territory. He sent them to the riverside settlement of Fort St. Gabriel. **9** And for a small amount of money, he gave each family some land, six hens, one rooster, one cow, some corn, and a musket with gunpowder and bullets.

When the Brasseux family reached St. Gabriel, they found a land like none they had ever seen before. But it was a place where they were free—free to speak French, free to worship as Catholics, free to live as Acadians. It was a place where they could make a home.

prosperous lives in the French colony. But now Nova Scotia belonged to Great Britain. 'You will swear allegiance to our king and give up your Catholic religion,' British officials told the Acadians. When they refused, the British decided to get rid of them once and for all. Besides, the officials wanted the Acadians' rich farms for themselves.

When the soldiers released the men and boys from the church, the Acadians' crops had been destroyed by fire and their families turned out of their homes. As would happen over and over again for the next five years, the Acadian prisoners were marched to waiting British ships. **4** Shoved below deck, crowded on top of one another, the Brasseux family gave thanks that they had at least managed to stay together. In the dark hold of the vessel, they could not see the soft green fields of Acadia sloping down to the sea. They could say goodbye only in their hearts.

Along the coast of the British colonies, the ships dropped off the exiles who had not died of disease and starvation on the overcrowded vessels. Elizabeth, Cosme, and their five children found themselves with hundreds of other Acadians, stranded on the shores of the Maryland colony. **5** They had no food, no shelter, and no welcome from the British colonists of Maryland.

For twelve years Elizabeth Brasseux struggled to keep her family together. No longer prosperous landowners, Cosme, Elizabeth, and their older children worked as laborers for whatever small wage they could

---

ACADIAN FACTS

■ *Acadians call the exile from Nova Scotia Le Grand Dérangement, which means "the great trouble" in French.*

■ *Scholars believe that 12,000 to 18,000 Acadians lived in Nova Scotia in 1755. By 1760 as many as 7,000 had been removed by the British and forced to resettle. Others fled to isolated areas in Canada, to France, and to French islands in the Caribbean.*

On the Forbidden Path

1760

Teedyuscung, the Delaware Indian chief, stood tall before the governor and council of the Pennsylvania colony. "You know that our hands are joined together, and we are entered into close Alliance and Friendship with each other," Teedyuscung reminded the officials. The chief was well known to be a peacemaker as the British and French fought to take over the land. Now he was to represent Pennsylvania at a great treaty meeting in the Ohio country. The governor asked Teedyuscung to convince all of the Indian people "to enter into the peace." **1** He also directed him to find and return white captives taken by the Indians.

Teedyuscung went home to prepare for the long journey west. A month later, the diplomat Frederick Post set out to join him. "You will give the Indians everywhere the strongest assurances that no person shall be permitted to make Settlements on their land," the governor had directed Post. Post rode to nearby Bethlehem, **2** where a companion, John Hays, joined him. Together, they proceeded past Fort Allen **3** to Wyoming, Teedyuscung's village. **4**

There, Teedyuscung and his wife were preparing for the chief's long absence—mending fences, planting corn, and putting aside food. Teedyuscung, Post, and Hays worked to make the wampum that they would take with them—strings and belts of shell beads used to carry symbolic messages in the Indian world. As they talked, Post showed Teedyuscung the letter the governor had received from General Sir Jeffrey Amherst, commander of all the British forces in North America. Amherst had a warning for the Indians: "If they do not behave as good and faithful allies ought to do, and renounce all Acts of Hostility against His Majesty's Subjects, I shall retaliate upon them." Teedyuscung knew what British retaliation meant. He feared that Amherst's harsh words would cause the Indians "to draw back instead of coming nigh."

Soon the group—now 14 in all—set out for the treaty meeting. In two days they came to a large Indian town, **5** where Teedyuscung and Post spoke of peace as "durable as the Mountains & to last as long as Sun & Moon give Light." The people of the town brought them three captives—two children and a young woman—whom Teedyuscung and Post promised to return to their homes.

Past the town the group crossed the swift Susquehanna River to the start of the Forbidden Path. **6** The path and the land around it were the sacred hunting grounds of the Iroquois Indians, forbidden territory to all white men. Teedyuscung was determined to take Post and Hays along, however. He sent strings of wampum as a message to the Iroquois upriver, asking them to meet for a council. Then they camped for the night at Aschkokuckwawealochtet, "a hole where snakes harbour." **7**

Along the Forbidden Path, the men learned of a great meeting between thousands of French and Indian people in Canada. Teedyuscung was more determined than ever to bring his message from the British to the

Fort Oswego

Onandaga

TEEDYUSCUNG FACTS

■ *The struggle for control of the Ohio Valley was at the heart of the French and Indian War. When the war ended in 1763, Great Britain controlled most of North America.*

■ *Although the British called Teedyuscung's people "the Delaware," they called themselves Lenni Lenape, which means "the people."*

---

mung R. **7**
Aschkokuck-
wawealochtet
Tioga
6
5
Wyalusing
Susquehanna North Branch
4
Wyoming
3
Fort Allen
2
Bethlehem
NEW JERSEY
1
Philadelphia

Delaware River

ATLANTIC OCEAN

N

0   15
Miles

---

treaty meetings. At the Munsee Indian town of Assinisink, **8** they came upon a great religious ceremony. For days, men and women sang and danced, turning their faces to the rising sun. On the fourth day, a messenger arrived from the Iroquois. The news was not what Teedyuscung wanted to hear. Not only would the Iroquois not come downriver for a council, they threatened to roast the white men alive. White men should not be on the Forbidden Path, the Indians warned.

Teedyuscung and Post had to decide. Should they, could they, go farther together? Finally they decided to go on to Secaughcung. **9** There, representatives of seven nations were gathered: Mingoes, Senecas, Shawnees, Fox, Unamis, Munsees, and Mahikans. Post addressed the council. Then Teedyuscung addressed the council. "We will help establish the Peace" with the English, the Indians promised. But they would not allow the white men to go any farther into the Ohio country. Finally, Frederick Post and John Hays mounted their horses to return to Philadelphia. As he left, Post wished Teedyuscung "all of the necessary Strength & Wisdom he stood in need of."

Teedyuscung would go on to the great treaty meeting. But no amount of strength and wisdom could change the future for his people. What Teedyuscung had hoped—to guarantee their freedom to live undisturbed—would not happen. Within three years the Delaware would have lost their lands forever.

DEBORAH SAMPSON FACTS

■ Robert Shurtliff Sampson was the name of Deborah's older brother, who died before she was born.

■ About six months after she returned home, Deborah Sampson married Benjamin Gannett, a farmer. They had three children. Deborah Sampson Gannett died in 1827 at the age of 66.

■ The U.S. Congress said of Deborah Sampson, "The whole history of the American Revolution records no case like this, and furnishes no other similar example of female heroism, fidelity, and courage."

Fort Ticonderoga

10

11

NEW YORK

NEW HAMPSHIRE

Connecticut River

9

Hudson River

MASSACHUSETTS

4

Worcester

3

Boston

Middleborough

1

Delaware River

West Point

5

8

CONNECTICUT

RHODE ISLAND

2

New Bedford

14

White Plains

7

LONG ISLAND

PENNSYLVANIA

New York

6

NEW JERSEY

13

Philadelphia

12

ATLANTIC OCEAN

N

0   20   40
Miles

Soldier in Disguise

1782

The recruiting officer stared at the tall young man who was asking to sign up as a soldier in the Continental army. The Revolutionary War was nearing an end—the British had already surrendered at Yorktown—but the conflict was not over, and General Washington was calling for more volunteers. Still, this young man did not look old enough to fight. Clearly he had not even grown a beard yet, the officer observed. When the young man said that he was 17, the officer relented. He recorded the date—May 20, 1782—and watched the recruit sign his name. *Robert Shurtliff*, the young man wrote, as he enlisted for three years in the Fourth Massachusetts Regiment of the Continental army.

In fact, the young recruit was not Robert Shurtliff at all. The recruit was a woman, 22-year-old Deborah Sampson, disguised as a man. Deborah Sampson had secretly sewed herself an outfit of men's clothing and cut her long blond curls to the length at which men wore their hair. **1** Dressed in her new clothes, she left the house. **2** Then Deborah did what she'd set out to do: she joined the army. **3** Deborah Sampson believed in independence —for herself and for the new United States. As a woman in those days, she had almost no freedom, but disguised as a man, she had plenty.

With 50 other recruits, Deborah made a 200-mile march **4** from Worcester, Massachusetts, to the fort at West Point, New York. At West Point **5** she learned to be a good soldier—so good that she was assigned to a special ranger unit.

Loyalists—Americans who remained loyal to Britain—were making trouble all over New York. Unwilling to accept Britain's defeat, they had occupied New York City. **6** So Deborah's unit was sent into enemy territory to spy. Near White Plains, when they were attacked by a group of Loyalists and British soldiers, **7** one musket ball passed right through Deborah's hat and another through her sleeve. In the next battle,

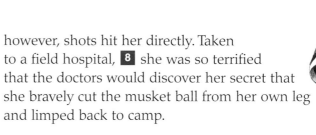

however, shots hit her directly. Taken to a field hospital, **8** she was so terrified that the doctors would discover her secret that she bravely cut the musket ball from her own leg and limped back to camp.

Deborah hated the stubborn Loyalists and soon took her revenge. After a wealthy Loyalist landowner refused food and water to Deborah and a dying soldier, she led a group of soldiers back to the man's house. They returned to camp with 20 Loyalist prisoners, nine horses, and the body of the dead soldier. On another mission, Deborah almost drowned in an icy river. (She may have been brave, but she did not know how to swim.)

That winter, Deborah was part of a regiment sent to upstate New York. **9** There they battled Mohawk Indians who were fighting to keep their land. **10** For two months the regiment faced the dangers of frostbite, wolves, **11** and bears. The soldiers showed "distinguished bravery," General Schuyler said.

Finally, the war was over, the peace treaty signed. Deborah Sampson had more adventures to come, however. Sent to Philadelphia to squash an uprising of angry veterans demanding back pay, **12** Deborah was struck by a deadly fever. When the doctor treated "Private Robert Shurtliff," **13** he discovered Deborah Sampson's secret. Recognizing the young soldier's bravery and determination, the doctor did not reveal her true identity to the other soldiers. Instead, he gave her a letter to turn over to her commanding officer.

When Deborah reached the fort, she presented the letter to General Paterson. **14** As he read this note revealing the truth about his soldier Robert Shurtliff, the general was astounded. How could a young woman have suffered and accomplished all that Deborah Sampson had? 'I wanted to serve my country,' the young soldier said simply. And then Deborah Sampson went home.

Called by the Voice of America

1789

Just after noon on an early spring day—April 14, 1789—a messenger on horseback galloped up to the plantation home of General George Washington. Charles Thomson arrived at Mount Vernon bearing the news that Washington had been unanimously elected the first president of the United States. "You are called by the voice of America," Thomson said.

George Washington did not want to leave home. The Virginia countryside had never looked lovelier, as the sheep clustered in the green fields and the dogwood blossoms floated gently in the air. Washington had left this home to fight for England against the French. And he had left it again to lead the armies battling for America's freedom. "No man should scruple or hesitate a moment . . . in defense of so valuable a blessing," he said. Now he was called in the name of freedom once more. The new nation could not survive without his leadership, he was told.

And so, on April 16 at ten in the morning, Washington said goodbye to his dear wife, Martha, and his beloved Mount Vernon. **1** As the carriage pulled away, he "bade adieu to Mount Vernon, to private life, and to domestic felicity," as he wrote in his diary.

GEORGE WASHINGTON FACTS

■ *Washington's journey from Mount Vernon to New York was 235 miles long and took seven days.*

■ *Martha Washington traveled from Mount Vernon to New York in May, with her grandchildren.*

Schuylkill River

Philade

Chester

Wilmington

4

5

PENNSYLVANIA

MARYLAND

Susquehanna River

NEW JERSEY

Baltimore

3

Chesapeake Bay

DELAWARE

Delaware Bay

Potomac River

Annapolis

Georgetown

Alexandria

2

1

Mount
Vernon

VIRGINIA

Crowds cheered Washington along the road and at every stop. From Spurrier's Tavern men on horseback led his carriage through throngs of admirers into Baltimore. There, at Mr. Grant's tavern, were more toasts, more speeches, and a supper fit for the man they called "Your Excellency." **3**

To enter Philadelphia two days later, Washington rode an elegant white horse. Leading a joyous procession of officials, soldiers, and citizens, he arrived at Gray's Ferry to cross the Schuylkill River. The small bridge spanning the river was decked with branches of laurel and evergreen. As Washington rode under a flowered arch at one end, 15-year-old Angelica Peale lowered a laurel wreath above his honored—and surprised—head. **4**

Bells pealed as Washington rode into Philadelphia **5** later that morning. By three o'clock he was dining at the City Tavern. The next morning he rode toward Assumpink Creek, **6** where a touching scene awaited him. The women of Trenton wanted to thank the general who had saved their city in war and the president who would lead the new nation. Mothers and daughters stood below a banner declaring, "The Defender of the Mothers Will Be the Protector of the Daughters." Deeply touched, George Washington passed under the archway as 6 little girls and 13 young ladies sang, "Welcome, mighty Chief! Once more, Welcome to this grateful shore . . ."

Two days later, on April 23, George Washington boarded a gaily decorated barge to cross the Hudson River from New Jersey to New York. As 13 sailors rowed the barge into the bay, they were joined by other boats. Flags were flying and crowds were cheering as the barge docked at Murray's Wharf in Manhattan. **7**

On April 30 the city's church bells began to ring at nine in the morning. By twelve-thirty the ceremonial procession began its journey through the flag-draped streets jammed with excited citizens. "He deserves it all," people cried out as Washington passed in his stagecoach. At Federal Hall, Vice President John Adams formally presented George Washington to both houses of Congress. A short while later, George Washington took the oath of office on the balcony outside. "God bless our president," the crowds roared.

Alexandria, Virginia, **2** was the first stop on the trip to New York, the nation's temporary capital. At Mr. Wise's tavern, neighbors waited to honor the president-elect. Raising their glasses, they toasted the people of the United States of America, the king of France, the memory of fallen heroes, the American ladies—13 toasts in all.

Buying Freedom

1795

Out on the South Carolina frontier, young Frank McWhorter was moving west. As he looked around the small wilderness farm **1** where he was born and grew up, Frank was not sorry to leave. The 18-year-old thought of the years of exhausting work—clearing land, plowing fields, harvesting crops. And he remembered the years of terror, as colonists and soldiers killed one another in the bloody fighting of the American Revolution. That revolution freed the United States, but it did not free Frank McWhorter. Frank was an African American slave.

Now Frank's owner, George McWhorter, was going west to settle the nation's new frontier in Kentucky. He sent Frank ahead with other pioneers **2** on the dangerous journey through the Cumberland Gap. **3** As the travelers struggled across the Appalachian Mountains on the narrow Wilderness Trace, they were under constant threat of attack from American Indians. The Indians rightly feared that the new settlers were going to seize their land. The journey was only 200 miles long, but it took Frank's wagon train a month to reach the Pennyroyal frontier in Kentucky.

Life in Kentucky was even harder. To set up his owner's new home, Frank chopped down trees and cleared the land. He fenced in fields and planted corn. And he guarded the farm from Indian attack. Frank also met and married Lucy, with whom he would share his life for the next 55 years. **4** Lucy, too, was a slave, owned by a master in another settlement. Within a year, Frank was a father, a father deeply determined to gain freedom for his family.

Good workers like Frank were prized on the frontier, and George McWhorter hired him out to other pioneers who needed help. Frank saw his chance. By working extra time, he was allowed to earn money for himself. If he could save enough, he realized, he could buy his

family's freedom. So Frank set out to do just that. In the caves around the McWhorter farm were the resources for making saltpeter, the main ingredient in gunpowder. So Frank set up a saltpeter business. **5** As long as Frank gave McWhorter the money he required, the owner allowed his slave to save money for himself. It took Frank years of work, but in 1817 he was able to buy the freedom of his beloved Lucy. Two years later, with Lucy's help, he had saved enough to buy himself from slavery. From that moment on, Frank McWhorter called himself Free Frank.

Free Frank was a good businessman, so good that he was able to buy the saltpeter business for himself. When the business was valuable enough, in 1829, he traded it for the freedom of his oldest son, Young Frank. Then Free Frank and Lucy decided it was time to leave Kentucky. Kentucky was a "slave state," but in many other states slavery was outlawed. So Free Frank and Lucy bought land in the "free state" of Illinois. In the fall of 1830 they set out for a new life with Young Frank and with their children born in

WISCONSIN

ILLINOIS

MICHIG

INDIAI

C

New Philadelphia, 1850

11

10

12

9

Mississippi River

KEN

TENN

O

freedom—Squire, Commodore, and Lucy. Tearfully, they left behind three children who were still in slavery—Juda, Sally, and Solomon. 'I will buy your freedom,' their father promised. **6**

Always fearful of the slave catchers **7** who captured African Americans—even free blacks—Free Frank and his family traveled in a great covered wagon. They chose their river crossings **8** carefully, always trying to avoid places where slave catchers were known to operate. Moving west, they crossed the state line into Illinois, with their cattle trailing behind the wagon. **9** By late December, though, blizzards made travel impossible. **10** Trapped in "the winter of the deep snow," Free Frank and his family barely survived. Finally, in April, they reached Pike County, where they would make their new home.

Slavery lay just 15 miles away, across the Mississippi River in Missouri. So almost immediately Free Frank went to the county seat to register his family as free blacks, legally purchased from slavery. Then Free Frank and Lucy and their children set to work building a house and a farm. **11** They planted 80 acres of wheat and corn and soon were raising cattle and hogs. By 1835 Free Frank had enough money to buy the freedom of his son Solomon and to bring him from Kentucky.

Still, Free Frank did not stop, for there were children and grandchildren left in slavery in Kentucky. On land that he had been buying little by little, Free Frank founded a town. He called it New Philadelphia. **12** By selling land in the town to new settlers, Free Frank was able to free his daughters and grandchildren from slavery. As he looked at his farm and his town, Free Frank was proud. But nothing in his life would make him as proud as buying the freedom of his family.

FREE FRANK FACTS

■ *In 1795, when Free Frank left South Carolina, about 5,000 settlers traveled the Wilderness Trace into Kentucky.*

■ *According to the laws of slavery, children born to a free mother were free. By buying Lucy's freedom first, Frank ensured that their future children would be born free.*

■ *The money that Free Frank earned purchased freedom for a total of 15 family members, plus himself.*

| Date of Freedom | Lucy 1817 | Free Frank 1819 | Juda 1850 | Frank 1829 | Sally 1843 | Solomon 1835 | Lucy Ann, Squire, Commodore born free | Permilla, Commodore, Louisa, Calvin 1850 | Calvin, Robert, Lucy Ann, Charlotte 1856 and children |

"Give Us Free!"

1839

Margru screamed in terror. Chaos surged around the little girl as she tried to hide on the deck of *La Amistad*. The African men had already killed the ship's captain and the cook. Now two sailors were escaping over the side into a small boat. As Margru and the three other African children on board watched, the African men took over the ship. They tied up the two Spanish men who had bought them as slaves just a few days before. And they threw the dead into the sea.

Sengbe Pieh was in charge now. It was Sengbe who had found the nail that the Africans used to open the chains that bound them. It was Sengbe who had quieted the children as the men crept up onto the deck. And it was Sengbe who now ordered the Spaniard Pedro Montes to sail them home to Africa.

Home! Thinking about the families and places they had left behind was almost more than the men and children could bear. Months before, they had been snatched away from everything they knew and loved. **1** Marched to the coast by slave catchers, they had been sold to slave traders, who threw them into cages called *barracoons*. **2** After spending two months in the *barracoons*, Sengbe, Margru, and hundreds of others were shipped across the Atlantic on a slave schooner. **3** Conditions on the ship were so foul, so inhuman, that many captives died—so many that sharks followed the ship, waiting for the dead bodies to be tossed overboard.

In Cuba, the Africans had been sold once again. **4** Sengbe, Margru, and 51 other Africans had been purchased by two Spaniards: Pedro Montes bought the 4 children and Jose Ruiz bought 49 men. The Spaniards loaded their human

purchases onto the *Amistad* to travel home along the coast of Cuba. But all of this changed on the July night when the Africans revolted. **5**

Each day after the revolt, Pedro Montes steered the ship east, toward Africa, as Sengbe ordered. **6** At night, however, Montes changed direction. Secretly, he was trying to sail the ship back to Cuba. But the winds blew the *Amistad* north along the coast of the United States. By late August the ship was off Long Island. **7** There, U.S. officials seized the *Amistad*, certain that it was the ship they had been

looking for. (Word of the *Amistad* revolt had reached the United States from Cuba, where the two sailors who escaped had told their story.)

Now the questioning began. For Sengbe, Margru, and the other Africans, it was a time of fear and confusion. In a language they could not understand, they were accused of murder and piracy. Pedro Montes and Jose Ruiz said the Africans were slaves and belonged to them. The Spanish government, too, said the Africans were slaves, property like the blankets and guns and soap also on the *Amistad*. The ship, the "murderers," and the cargo must be returned to their owners, they said. Americans who owned slaves agreed. But many others did not. Soon, American abolitionists—people who wanted to abolish slavery—took up the cause of the *Amistad* captives.

As arguments swirled around them, the African men were put in jail. **8** The children—Margru, Teme, Kagne, and Kali—were taken into the home of the jailers, Colonel and Mrs. Pendleton. Newspapers were filled with reports about the African captives. Americans filed through the jail to look at them. Abolitionists collected money to help them. And a local professor began to search for someone who could understand them.

On September 19, 1839, the first court case was decided in New Haven. An American court could not try the Africans for murder or piracy, the judge said, for the events had not happened in American waters. But still the Africans were not free. Another court, another judge, would decide whether they should be sent back to slavery or sent home to Africa. In jail, Sengbe and the other men talked among themselves. 'What will happen to us? Will we never be free?' they asked. But no one understood. Then one day James Covey, a free African man, was brought to the jail. He spoke to them in Mende, a language they all understood. With shouts of joy, the men began to talk and talk and talk. At last they could tell their story and people would understand.

On a cold November day in Hartford, Sengbe went to court for the next trial. **9** With Covey to translate, he told the story of the *Amistad* and its captives. He told of the terrors they had faced, and he asked for their freedom. "Give us free! Give us free!" Sengbe cried.

There would be still another trial, in the U.S. Supreme Court, but finally the men and the children of the *Amistad* were given back their freedom. On November 25, 1841, Margru and Sengbe and the others sailed for Africa. As those who had helped them waved goodbye, they went home, free. **10**

AMISTAD FACTS

■ La Amistad *means "friendship" in Spanish.*

■ *In 1839 it was illegal for Americans to import slaves into the United States. But slavery itself was legal in half of the nation. Slavery was not fully outlawed in the United States until 1865, after the Civil War.*

■ *Margru later came back to the United States, attended Oberlin College, and returned to Africa to become the principal of a school.*

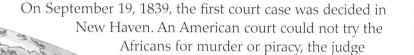

EUROPE

AFRICA

C OCEAN

Margru   Sengbe

A Thousand Miles for Freedom

1848

As dawn lit the sky over the Georgia planta-tion, **1** William Craft cut off his wife's long hair. Quickly, Ellen Craft finished putting on the jacket and trousers that William had brought her. She wrapped a large handkerchief around her pale, beardless face and put on a pair of green eyeglasses so that she would look even less like herself. William studied her disguise carefully. "You make a most respectable-looking gentleman," he said. "Come, my dear," William whispered as he took Ellen's hand, "let us make a desperate leap for liberty!"

Just a few days earlier, the Crafts had come up with a daring plan to escape from slavery. Ellen Craft was so light-skinned that she could pass for white. Disguised as an invalid, she would pretend to be a white man—"Mr. Johnson"—traveling with his slave, William. At daybreak this December morning, William and Ellen Craft left the plantation separately. Though "Mr. Johnson" had no trouble, William was questioned. **2**

Frightened but determined, the Crafts finally reached the station and boarded the train for Savannah. **3** "Mr. Johnson" sat down in a railroad car reserved for whites, while William was sent to a car for slaves. When "Mr. Johnson" realized that the man sitting next to her had known her since childhood, she was terrified. But her disguise worked. "It's a very fine morning, sir," the man said.

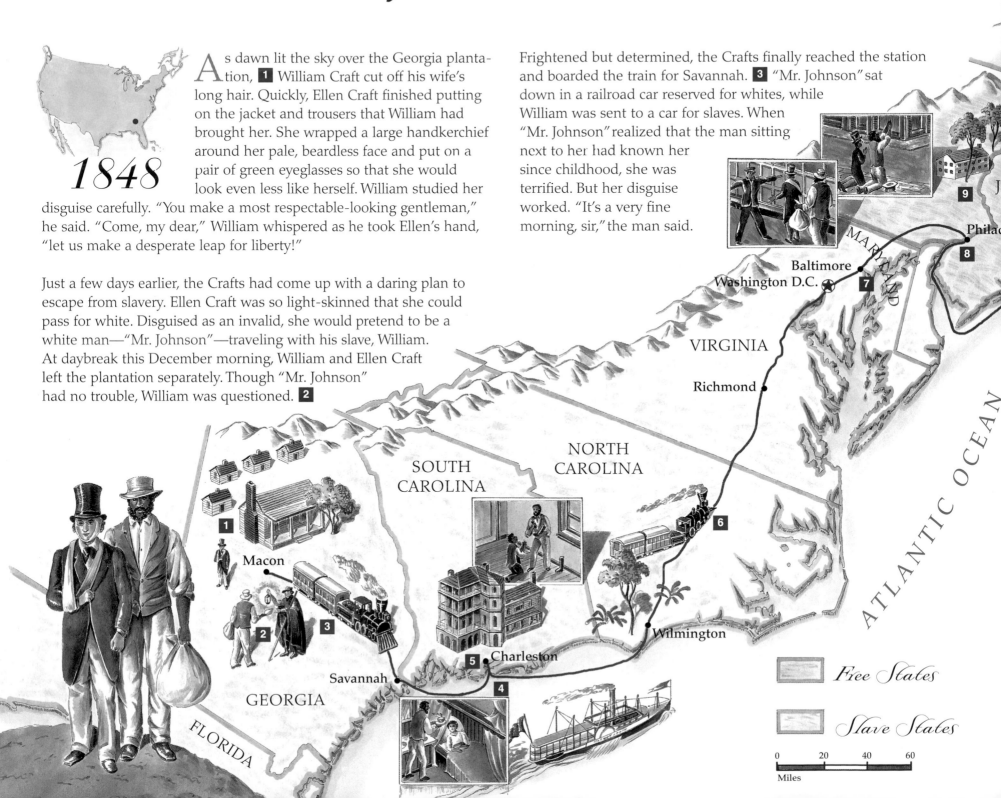

ATLANTIC OCEAN

MARYLAND

Baltimore
Washington D.C.
Philad

VIRGINIA

Richmond

NORTH CAROLINA

SOUTH CAROLINA

Wilmington

Charleston

Macon

Savannah

GEORGIA

FLORIDA

Free States

Slave States

0   20   40   60
Miles

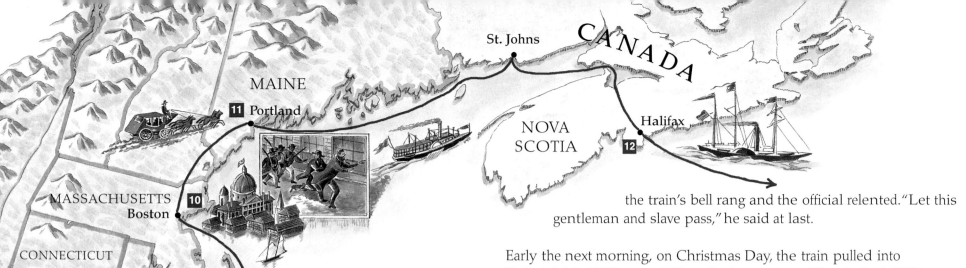

the train's bell rang and the official relented. "Let this gentleman and slave pass," he said at last.

Early the next morning, on Christmas Day, the train pulled into Philadelphia. William and Ellen Craft were free. "Thank God, William, we are safe!" Ellen cried as they knelt down, in tears. **8** Supporters working to abolish slavery, however, worried that Philadelphia was too close to slave states for them to be safe. A kindly Quaker family took William and Ellen to their home in the country **9** until arrangements could be made for them to go to Boston.

For almost two years, the Crafts made a new life in Boston. Then, in 1850, the U.S. Congress passed the Fugitive Slave Bill. Suddenly, any escaped slave anywhere could be sent back to slavery. In a short time the people who had owned William and Ellen Craft sent men to Boston to bring them back to Georgia. But this was not to be. It seemed as though all of Boston rose up against the slave catchers. A Vigilance Committee guarded William at the Crafts' home. Others took Ellen away to safety. Finally, the slave catchers fled, pursued by the Vigilance Committee. **10** Meanwhile, friends made plans to take the Crafts to safety. They went first by carriage to Maine **11**, then to New Brunswick in Canada. Steamers took them on to Nova Scotia. In Halifax, William and Ellen Craft boarded a ship for England. **12** Not until after the Civil War was over and slavery was outlawed in the nation would they return.

By evening, "Mr. Johnson" and William were aboard a ship **4** to Charleston. Afraid of being discovered, "Mr. Johnson" went to her cabin right away. When William followed, pretending to bring medicines, the couple could at last talk in private. William took such good care of his "master" that a slave dealer on board wanted to buy him. "I don't wish to sell, sir," "Mr. Johnson" said quickly.

In Charleston, William helped "Mr. Johnson" to a hotel while they waited for the next ship. There, he met another enslaved man, Pompey. **5** Learning that William was on his way to Philadelphia, Pompey said that he had heard there was no slavery there. "When you gets de freedom," Pompey said, tears running down his face, "don't forget to pray for poor Pompey."

Another ship took "Mr. Johnson" and William to North Carolina, where they boarded a train going north. **6** They made their way to Baltimore. **7** There, on Christmas Eve, their flight to freedom almost ended. As they boarded the train to Philadelphia, officials demanded that "Mr. Johnson" prove his right to take his slave into the free state of Pennsylvania. "You have no right to detain us here," "Mr. Johnson" cried out. "Well, sir, right or no right, we shan't let you go," the official replied. To "Mr. Johnson" and William, the words felt like "the crack of doom." A crowd had gathered around the silent invalid and the slave. Suddenly

---

WILLIAM AND ELLEN CRAFT FACTS

■ *The Crafts traveled throughout Great Britain, where slavery had been abolished in 1835. They told the famous story of their escape and preached against slavery.*

■ *In 1869, four years after the end of the Civil War, the Crafts returned to Georgia to set up a cooperative farm for freedmen.*

Walking to Zion

1856

Peter McBride was tired of waiting. To the six-year-old boy, the months since he had left his home in Scotland seemed an eternity. Peter and his parents were Mormons, members of the Church of Jesus Christ of Latter-day Saints. Nine years earlier, American Mormon leaders had created a haven in Utah, where Mormons could worship free from persecution. They called it Zion. Along with thousands of other Saints, the McBrides left Europe, sailed to America, and took a train to the banks of the Mississippi River. **1** There, Mormon organizers were ready to help them follow their dreams to Zion.

For weeks, the McBrides had lived in a sea of tents near Iowa City. **2** Without money to buy a covered wagon, Peter's father and others built handcarts to carry their belongings. On July 26, 576 Saints set out, led by Captain Edward Martin. **3** Peter walked alongside while his father pulled and pushed the cart, with its 400 pounds of supplies. It was the beginning of a 1,400-mile walk.

Struggling with broken carts and heavy loads, it took the Martin handcart company six weeks to reach the Missouri River, three weeks longer than they had planned. After they ferried across the big, dirty river, **4** they started over the Great Plains. The hardship mounted in unusually cold weather. "The scarcity of food and wood caused many strong men to perish," Peter McBride remembered. **5** Still, the Saints pushed on. "Our faith and arms with a right good will, Shall pull our carts along," they sang. Some days they had nothing to eat but flour. Other times one of the oxen died and there was meat. "We had to burn buffalo chips for wood . . . not a tree in sight," Peter marveled.

Ahead lay the mountains, but first the travelers had to cross the North Platte River. **6** At Last Crossing the river was shallow but wide. It was so cold that chunks of ice

Great Salt Lake

South Pass

Sweetwater

7

6

8

ROCKY MOUNTAINS

Fort Laramie

Chimney Rock

Scott's Bluff

North Platte

9

Salt Lake City

N

0   50   100
Miles

floated down the river as the travelers dragged and floated their carts across. A Mormon wagon train had caught up with the handcart company and was able to help them across the river. Peter rode with Cyrus Wheelock on a horse. "I slid off in the shallow water. I held on to the horse's tail and came out all right," Peter remembered. Young Patience Loader almost drowned when she waded in. "Mother was standing on the bank screaming as we got near . . . for God's Sake some of you men help my poor girls." And the men did, some crossing the river 75 times that day to get the carts and travelers across.

Later, in camp, it was hard for the travelers to remember the faith that had brought them there. Peter McBride's father died that night. When they pushed on the next day, the handcart company left 13 buried in the snowdrift beside the trail.

The journey only got worse. Finally, the travelers held a meeting. "It was decided that we could go no further, the snow so deep and no food. We were doomed to starvation," Peter said. When he woke up the next morning, the snow had drifted over his tent and his hair was frozen to the canvas. Just when all seemed lost, they heard a joyous shout. Relief had come, wagons with food and clothing from Utah. **7** "Surely they are angels from heaven," a young girl cried. In spite of the rescuers, many of the travelers would die in the icy days ahead. **8**

The Saints made one last push, 300 miles through the mountains. At Big Mountain Pass, they caught their first sight of Zion—Salt Lake City, the heart of their new world. **9** Some waved handkerchiefs and sang for joy. One woman pushed her handcart over the edge of a cliff and marched into Zion with her faith alone. For Peter, the moment was bittersweet as he remembered those lost along the way. It was an end and a beginning.

MORMON FACTS

■ *The Church of Jesus Christ of Latter-day Saints was founded in the United States in 1830. Within a few years, missionaries had traveled to Europe, where they converted families like the McBrides.*

■ *The 426 survivors in the Martin handcart company arrived in Salt Lake City on November 30, 1856, more than four months after they left Iowa City.*

Lake Michigan

Missouri River

• Chicago

Iowa City **2**

3

Kanesville **4**

5

Platte River

Mississippi River **1**

"For Honor, Duty, and Liberty"

1863

Henry Gooding's heart filled with pride as he marched along the streets of Boston toward the Battery Wharf. Everywhere, cheering crowds applauded the thousand African American soldiers in the uniform of the U.S. Army. "Can we believe our own eyes and ears?" a reporter exclaimed. "Is this Boston? Is it America?" The bitter Civil War between North and South had raged since 1860, but until recently only white soldiers had been allowed to fight in the Union army. Now the 54th Massachusetts Volunteer Infantry was on its way to war. Like Henry Gooding, some of the black soldiers had been born free. Others had escaped the slavery at the heart of the conflict. They fought "for honor, duty, and liberty," Henry Gooding said. They fought because "slavery must die."

All spring the men of the 54th had trained to be soldiers under the leadership of a young army colonel, Robert Gould Shaw. They had worked hard, and Gooding was confident that the 54th would be "a credit to old Massachusetts wherever it goes." That afternoon the soldiers boarded a ship for South Carolina. **1** Gooding, Shaw, and many of the others would never see Boston again.

The 54th joined other regiments camped on sea islands that had been conquered by the North. **2** The South was a new world for soldiers like Henry Gooding. The soldiers of the 54th had special reason to fear the rebels, for Southern armies had sworn either to kill black soldiers or to enslave them.

In a raid on the town of Darien, **3** the 54th met no enemy attack. But soon enough, the rebels made their presence known. Near dawn on July 16, Southern troops attacked the men on James Island. It was the 54th's first real battle, and, although greatly outnumbered, they "behaved gallantly," Gooding thought. "It is not for us to blow our horn; but when a regiment of white men gave us three cheers as we were passing them, it shows that we did our duty as men should."

The 54th's greatest moment, however, would come just two days later. Northern generals wanted to capture Fort Wagner, the giant earthworks that protected Charleston—630 feet wide, built of sand and logs, and heavily armed. The men of the 54th were exhausted after the battle of James Island and a treacherous night march across the marshes to reach Fort Wagner. But Colonel Shaw said yes when the general asked if the 54th would like to lead the assault. He believed it was an honor for his men that he could not turn down. At 7:45 on the night of July 18, 600 men and 22 officers of the 54th Massachusetts Volunteers led the advance on Fort Wagner. **4** "Take the fort or die there," Shaw had said. Advancing at "double quick," the men rushed across the sand toward the fort, their bayonets thrust ahead. Shots screamed through the air all around them. "Mortal men could not stand such a fire," Henry Gooding said. "They mowed us down like grass," another remembered. Always at the front was Colonel Shaw, to the moment when he reached the top of the fort wall. "Forward, 54th," he shouted. And then he fell, shot dead.

Bravely as the Northern soldiers fought, they were so outnumbered and the fort so strong that their armies retreated from the battle. Of the men of the 54th, 256 soldiers and 14 officers perished at Fort Wagner. Henry Gooding was one who survived. For the next six months the remainder of the 54th joined other regiments in the siege of Charleston. **5** When they were unable to capture the city, the armies were ordered to action in Florida. There, at the bloody battle of Olustee, Henry Gooding was wounded and captured. **6** He was taken to the dreaded prison camp at Andersonville, Georgia.

The 54th Massachusetts Volunteers continued to fight to the very end of the war, firing their final shots in celebration of the peace. Henry Gooding dreamt of that day: "What a country this will be to live in, when the Star of Peace reigns once more supreme, and that bane of its life, slavery, will only be known in history!" But he did not live to see it. Henry Gooding died at Andersonville on July 19, 1864.

SOUTH CAROLINA

Charleston

James Island

Fort Wagner

ATLANTIC OCEAN

1

4

2

Savannah

N

0   20   40   60
Miles

Darien **3**

GEORGIA

Jacksonville

Suwanee River

6

Battle of Olustee

FLORIDA

MASSACHUSETTS 54TH FACTS

■ *The Civil War lasted from 1861 to 1865.*

■ *About 179,000 African American men joined the Union army. By the end of the war, one quarter of the Union navy was African American.*

■ *Henry Gooding wrote a series of letters to his hometown newspaper, the* New Bedford Mercury, *which printed them weekly between March 1863 and February 1864.*

Gold Mountain

SIERRA NEVADA

PACIFIC OCEAN

OREGON

CALIFORNIA

1 **2** Sacramento

Sacramento River

San Francisco

1865

Ah Goong did not want to leave home. He loved his family and his village, but times were hard in southeastern China. Too many floods, too many people, too many taxes. 'Go to Gam Saan,' his wife said. 'Go to Gold Mountain. Make money.' Ah Goong had heard about America, had heard the stories of mountains made of gold. For more than ten years men from China had gone to California to find work—and sometimes gold. So Ah Goong left home, boarded a ship, and sailed to California. He prayed that with the money he earned there, he could free his family from a life of poverty.

More than two months later, Ah Goong arrived in San Francisco. **1** Thousands of Chinese men were already there, some to stay, others on their way to the Sierra Nevada mountains. Hearing that there was work building a railroad, Ah Goong headed for the mountains. Outside Sacramento, **2** he was hired for a dollar a day to work on the brand-new Central Pacific line. At that moment, the young Chinese man became part of a great project that would change the entire United States. Starting in Omaha, Nebraska, the Union Pacific line was laying tracks west. Starting in Sacramento, the Central Pacific was laying tracks east. When they met east of the Sierra Nevada, the nation would be connected by railroad from coast to coast.

Ah Goong began on a crew that cut down giant trees to make way for the train tracks. **3** One trunk was so huge that 100 men could stand on it at one time. Whenever he could, Ah Goong looked for gold—in the dirt, in mountain streams—and sometimes he found it. **4** At night he stared up at the stars and thought of his family. If only the railroad would take him home, he wished. But the next morning he would find himself in these far-off mountains, lonely and cold. So Ah Goong stayed, saving money to send home to his family.

After a few years, the railroad men decided to hire more Chinese men. They were hard workers, unafraid of the gunpowder used to explode through the mountain granite. **5**

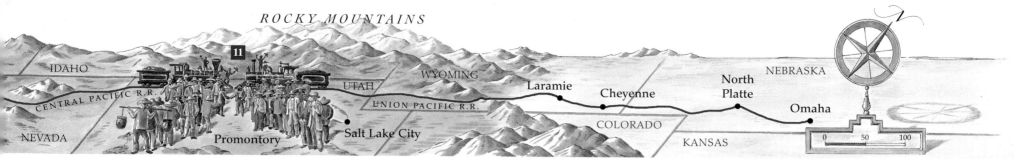

By the end of 1865, Ah Goong was one of 7,000 Chinese men on the Central Pacific crews. All that winter, he worked with his countrymen at the cliff called Cape Horn. The cliff was so narrow and so high that the Americans did not know how they could ever build tracks along it. But the Chinese men knew how, using a technique developed in China years earlier. Soon Ah Goong was being lowered over the side of the cliff with a rope around his waist. Swinging 1,200 feet above a rushing river, Ah Goong made a hole in the granite with a small drill, stuffed the hole with gunpowder, **6** and lit a fuse. Then he waved to the man high above to pull him up before the gunpowder exploded. From one spring to the next summer, the Chinese men swung over the cliff. Many died when they fell or were blown up, but Ah Goong survived.

Then came the tunnels. **7** There was no way around the highest peaks of the Sierra Nevada, so the men tunneled through the rock with hand drills, sledgehammers, and gunpowder. Ah Goong worked on the tunnels for two years. First shoveling dirt, then hammering granite, he pushed his way through the tunnel like a mole. The men worked eight-hour shifts, 24 hours a day. At the end of a day, they had moved just one foot forward. Then the bosses decided to use nitroglycerin as an explosive. Ah Goong saw explosions blow up 500-pound boulders— and kill workers at the same time. But still, Ah Goong survived.

In the winter of 1866–67, there was so much snow that the workers built snow tunnels to protect the trains, **8** as well as other tunnels where they could live ten feet below the surface. Finally, when the snow melted, the real tunnels—the railroad tunnels—were completed. It was then that the Chinese workers went on strike. **9** The bosses had offered them more money but for working more hours. The Chinese men planned the strike by sending notes to one another up and down the tracks, secretly wrapped in bundles of food. On June 25, 1867, Ah Goong and his countrymen stopped working. It took only nine days for the bosses to realize that they could not do without the Chinese workers, and work began again. **10** The strike was settled.

Almost two years later— in May 1869—a Central Pacific engine and a Union Pacific engine touched "noses" at Promontory, Utah. **11** As the last rails were put in place by Chinese workers, the transcontinental railroad was completed. Almost seven years after he landed in San Francisco, Ah Goong set out for home. On the way, he had some of the gold he had found made into a ring for his wife—a gold ring from Gold Mountain, where Ah Goong had helped change America.

AH GOONG FACTS

■ *Ah Goong was an ancestor of the American writer Maxine Hong Kingston. She told his story in her book* China Men.

■ *Until 1859, the emperor of China forbid anyone to leave the country. Leaving was a crime punishable by death. After gold was discovered in California in 1848, thousands of Chinese men secretly came to America to work.*

Flight of the Nez Perce

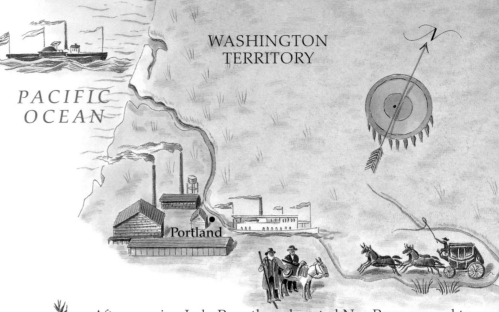

1877

These are our last days of freedom, Wetatonmi thought as she gathered food in the field. Fearing the future, she headed back to camp with her husband, Chief Ollokot, and his brother, Chief Joseph. Along with other Nez Perce Indians, they had been ordered to leave their homeland for a reservation. Newcomers—miners, farmers, ranchers—wanted their beloved Wallowa Valley, and the U.S. government had given it to them. The Nez Perce were like deer and the white men were like grizzly bears, Joseph said. He believed the Indians had no choice but to leave.

Wetatonmi slowed her horse as she saw Two Moons galloping toward their group. "War has broken out," he shouted wildly. Young Nez Perce warriors had struck out to revenge the murder of an elder. Now 15 whites were dead. Back at the camp, **1** the chiefs decided to flee to White Bird Canyon.

A few days later, on June 17, a coyote cry alerted the Nez Perce in the canyon. The U.S. soldiers had come. Hoping for peace, the Nez Perce sent out a truce party. But first one shot and then another cracked out from a scout's rifle, and in minutes 34 soldiers were killed. **2** No Indians died, but the Nez Perce knew that any hopes of peace were gone.

For days the Nez Perce families moved along the Salmon River ahead of the soldiers. Chief Looking Glass and his band had joined them after soldiers burned their village. **3** There were almost 700 in flight now—about 150 warriors and chiefs and the rest women, children, and old men who could no longer fight. With them were about 2,000 horses, the Nez Perces' most treasured possessions.

On July 11, the soldiers caught up with them at Clearwater. **4** Once again, the Nez Perce outfought them. Wetatonmi and other wives brought water and fresh horses into battle. For two days the warriors held off the soldiers so that the families could escape first.

After crossing Lolo Pass, the exhausted Nez Perce paused to rest at the Big Hole Valley. On August 9, as the families slept, the U.S. soldiers attacked. **5** Warriors struggled to arm themselves as gunfire flew "like hail and rain." A father cried out to his family to cross the creek and hide in the willows. Nearby a woman was killed in her tepee with her newborn baby. Wetatonmi survived, but of the 89 Nez Perce dead, more than 50 were women, children, and old people. It was a massacre.

Their only escape, the Nez Perce decided, was to reach Canada. They took flight through the mountains and across Yellowstone, the new national park. **6** As tourists fled, the Nez Perce and their horses pressed on.

Just 30 miles from the Canadian border, the exhausted Nez Perce made camp north of Bear's Paw. There, on September 30, the soldiers found them. In rain and then snow, the army sent deadly fire into the Nez Perce camp. One by one the chiefs were killed until only Chief Joseph and Chief White Bird were left. Finally Joseph surrendered, with more than 400 of his people. **7** "My heart is sick and sad," he said. "From where the sun now stands, I will fight no more forever."

Before Joseph surrendered, Wetatonmi fled to Canada with White Bird and about 200 others. **8** "It was lonesome, the leaving," she said. "Husband dead, friends buried or held prisoners. . . . Our going was with heavy hearts, broken spirits. But we would be free! Escaping the bondage sure with the surrendering. All lost, we walked silently on into the wintry night."

Chief Jose

BRITISH NORTH AMERICA (CANADA)

NEZ PERCE FACTS

■ *The flight of the Nez Perce covered 1,700 miles.*

■ *Those who surrendered with Chief Joseph were sent to the Oklahoma Territory, then sent to a reservation in the Northwest about eight years later. Chief Joseph was never allowed to see the Wallowa Valley again.*

■ *After a year or so, Wetatonmi and others left Canada and "wandered without a home." Eventually, she lived on the Nez Perce reservation. "Never surrendering, I have always been free," she said.*

MONTANA TERRITORY

Milk River

Missouri River

8

7

Bear Paw

chiefs' council

trading with settlers

Fort Lapwai

3

Nez Perce reservation

4

Wallowa Valley

2

Clearwater

Salmon River

Stevensville

White Bird Canyon

5

Big Hole

Yellowstone River

Battle of Canyon Creek

Crow Indians

6

Yellowstone National Park

tourists flee

WYOMING TERRITORY

Chief Looking Glass

stampeding army horses

Wetatonmi

0   25   50   75
Miles

The Promised Land

1894

"At last I was going to America! Really, really going, at last," Mary Antin cried when she heard the news. For three years since her father left for America, Mary had waited for this moment. Finally he was able to send the boat tickets. Now Hannah Antin and her children—Mary, Frieda, Deborah, and Joseph—were ready to leave their home in Russia. It seemed as though half the village of Polotzk had come to see them off. "May America shower gold coins on you," Hayye the wig maker said. "God help you!" "Goodbye!" "Remember . . ."the villagers called out as the train pulled away. **1**

Her mother was sad and a little frightened, but 13-year-old Mary was thrilled. Even as a child, Mary knew that life was hard in the Pale of Settlement, where Russian Jews were forced to live. And now she was headed for America, "the land of promise."

In Vilna the Antins stopped to bid farewell to Uncle Borris. On a rainy April morning, they waved goodbye and set out for the station in horse-drawn droshkies. **2** After their train left Versbolovo, Mary suddenly heard a frightening sound as a German doctor and several policemen stomped through the cars, questioning all of the Russian travelers. **3** They were looking for people who might have been exposed to the deadly disease cholera that was spreading in Russia. The Antins were healthy, but the policemen said that they could not travel without different tickets. 'We will take your passports and send you back to Polotzk,' the officers threatened.

Pointing to her four children, Hannah begged the officers to be kind. One of them was. 'Go to Herr Schidorsky in Kibart,' he said. 'He will help you.'

'Come, I will get you passes into Germany,' Herr Schidorsky told the worried Antins. Two days later they found themselves on yet another crowded train. **4** Mary remembered the "awkward bundles hugged in our arms, and our hearts set on America."

NORTH SEA

DENMARK

Hamburg

7

8

6

Berlin

Elbe River

GERMANY

Passing through the great city of Berlin, **5** Mary could not believe what she saw and heard. "Bells, whistles, hammers, locomotives shrieking madly, men's voices, peddlers' cries, horses hoofs, dogs' barkings. . . . We had never seen so large a city before." Outside Berlin the train stopped and all were rushed to a nearby house. People dressed in white hurriedly separated men and women, passengers and baggage. "Quick! Quick!" they shouted as they stripped and showered the passengers and threw their clothing into kettles of boiling water—all to get rid of any trace of the dreaded cholera. **6** At last, the family boarded yet another train, to Hamburg.

In Hamburg there was more questioning and disinfecting, more waiting. This time, the Antins found themselves in a prison near the North Sea. **7** For two weeks they waited in quarantine with hundreds of others. Mary could hear the sea, but she couldn't see it. "Our turn came at last," Mary said. "We found ourselves—we five frightened pilgrims from Polotzk—on the deck of a great big steamship afloat on the strange big waters of the ocean. For 16 days the ship was our world." **8**

It was 16 days of seasickness and fear for these travelers, who had never been on the ocean before. But Mary, ever adventurous, was deeply moved by "the deep solemn groans of the sea, sounding as if all the voices of the world had been turned into sighs." At last, on May 8, the *Polynesia* arrived in Boston. There, in "the Promised Land," Mr. Antin joyously greeted his family.

Everything seemed wondrous to Mary as she discovered America that summer. "Light was free. . . . Music was free. . . . Education was free," she exclaimed. Education, Mr. Antin explained, was "the treasure that no thief could touch." Finally, September came and he could give his children that great gift. When Mr. Antin stood before the teacher, his heart was full. "I think Miss Nixon guessed what my father's best English could not convey," Mary realized. "I think she divined that by the simple act of delivering our school certificates to her he took possession of America."

BALTIC SEA

RUSSIAN EMPIRE

Dvine River

Polotzk **1**

Versbolovo **3**

Vilna **2**

4

Vistula River

Oder River

MARY ANTIN FACTS

■ *Harsh rules restricted where Russian Jews could live, what they could do, and how they could worship. In the late 1800s many were allowed to live only in one part of Russia, called the Pale of Settlement. A "pale"—from the Latin word for "fence post"—was a restricted area.*

0 25 50 75 100
Miles

Going North

1924

Mildred Mack was *very* excited. Everything was about to change, and ten-year-old Mildred knew it. Today was July Fourth, the best day of the year, when the African American community in the town of North, South Carolina, got together for a big barbecue. People started cooking days ahead of time, baking cakes and pies, cooking beans, and barbecuing the meat. Mildred loved it all. But this year was different. Mildred had watched her mother quietly telling her friends goodbye. And now they were packing up everything in their little house. Minnie Mack, Mildred's mother, put all of their clothes in a big trunk as Mildred watched over her four younger brothers and sisters.

That night, a neighbor took the trunk away in his buggy. **1** The Macks were moving north. In May, Eddie Mack, Mildred's father, had left in the dark of night to catch the train to New Jersey. He wanted to get his family out of the South, but that wasn't such an easy thing to do. If you tried to board a train in North, "the white folks would stop you," he explained to Mildred. Some white people felt as though sharecroppers like Eddie Mack "belonged to them." In fact, the month before, Eddie Mack had sent his wife train tickets so the family could join him in New Jersey. But a white man opened the letter, took the tickets, and came to Minnie Mack's door. "Tell Eddie to come home where he belongs," the man told Mrs. Mack. She just nodded and didn't say much. Secretly, Minnie Mack had a plan.

On Saturday morning, July 5, Minnie Mack pulled down all of the shades in the house and locked the door so none of the white people in

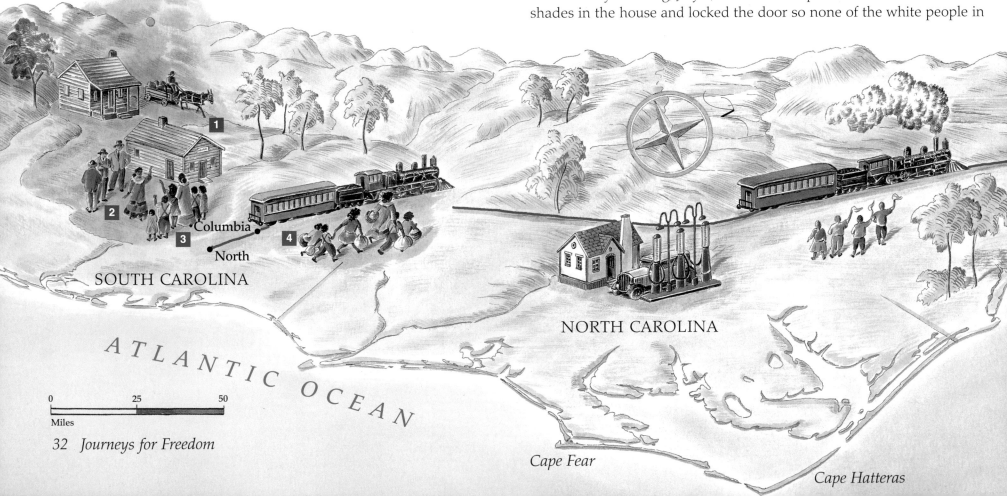

SOUTH CAROLINA

Columbia

North

NORTH CAROLINA

ATLANTIC OCEAN

0   25   50
Miles

Cape Fear

Cape Hatteras

town would know that the house was empty. Together, the family walked down to the train station. Aunt Rosa was waiting there, ready to help them fool the white people. "Yeah, we're going up to Columbia," Minnie Mack said. "I'll be glad to get up there and eat some of Minnie Durant's ice cream." On the train platform some of the white men in town were watching them. **2** They didn't know what Aunt Rosa and the Macks knew: Minnie Mack was not taking her family to nearby Columbia to eat ice cream. She was taking them there to catch the train to New Jersey.

 When the morning train pulled into North, the Macks hurried aboard the "colored car," the car reserved for black people. Mildred waved as Aunt Rosa called out, "Bye, I won't see you Sunday when you get back." **3**
Aunt Rosa knew that the Macks would not be back on Sunday. By then they would be in their new home "up north."

At eleven that morning the Macks arrived in Columbia. Right away, they went to Minnie Durant's home, where their trunk was waiting and where the Durants were ready to help them on their journey. Mr.

Durant went back to the station to buy them tickets on The Special, the train that ran north from Florida. Mrs. Durant filled a big basket with food: chicken, cakes, pies, enough to last the trip. At five in the evening, the Macks boarded The Special on its way north to Washington, D.C. **4**

When the train reached Washington **5** on Sunday afternoon, Minnie Mack finally felt safe. She had brought her family north. But only when the train pulled into Newark that evening did Mildred feel happy. "I was so glad to see my daddy that day," Mildred remembered later. "Lord, I was so glad to see my daddy." **6** When they walked out of Newark's Pennsylvania Station, Mildred could not believe her eyes. The whole city was lit with gaslights, something she had never seen before. Then Eddie Mack took his family on their first trolley-car ride, all the way up the avenue to their new house.

Mildred was glad to see their new home and to meet the Italian neighbors next door. But more than anything, she was glad to see the Newton Street School, right across the street. **7** "I want to go to that school," Mildred said. And so she did.

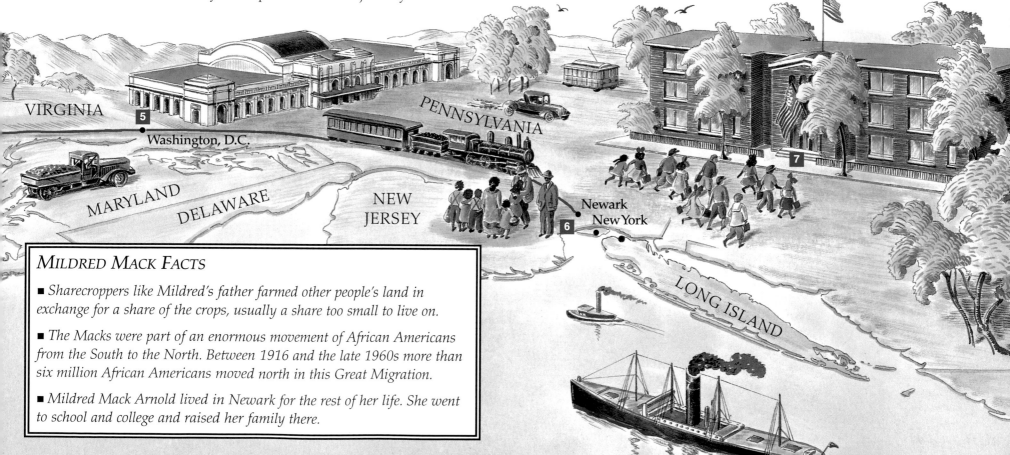

VIRGINIA
5 Washington, D.C.
MARYLAND
DELAWARE
NEW JERSEY
PENNSYLVANIA
Newark
New York
6
7
LONG ISLAND

MILDRED MACK FACTS

■ *Sharecroppers like Mildred's father farmed other people's land in exchange for a share of the crops, usually a share too small to live on.*

■ *The Macks were part of an enormous movement of African Americans from the South to the North. Between 1916 and the late 1960s more than six million African Americans moved north in this Great Migration.*

■ *Mildred Mack Arnold lived in Newark for the rest of her life. She went to school and college and raised her family there.*

The Road to California

1934

Lightning ripped out of the sky above the dusty Oklahoma plains and struck the barn on the Haggard farm. There had been no rain, no water, all year, and Flossie and James Haggard could not save their burning barn or the precious food that it contained. **1** As they looked around them, they knew that their lives had changed forever. It had been a terrible year, with a drought that turned the fields so dry they were like a bowl of dust. Their cotton crop failed. They sold their animals for as little as two cents a pound when they could feed them no longer. And now the fire.

Flossie and James were not quitters. They loved Oklahoma and wanted to stay. When they lost the farm, they took the children—Lowell and Lillian—and moved into town. In Checotah, **2** James tried to make a living for his family by running a filling station. Times were hard all over America in those days, and few people had much money for gasoline. Still, people were leaving Oklahoma in a stream of cars and trucks, heading along Route 66 to find work and new lives in California. Okies, they would be called.

Finally, the Haggards joined the exodus. On a blistering July day in 1935, Flossie, James, Lowell, and Lillian packed a few belongings and necessary supplies into their 1926 Chevrolet and the two-wheeled trailer James had rigged up behind it. Flossie patted the $40 in her pocket. It was all the money they had, sent by her sister, who had gone to California a year before. As they set out on Route 66, **3** Flossie said a special goodbye to her Oklahoma life. She had come there in a covered wagon from Arkansas when she was a child and when Oklahoma was still Indian Territory.

That night they slept along the side of the road. **4** For the children it was an adventure, but Flossie and James felt homeless and lonely.

Flossie baked bread in a little Dutch oven and carefully portioned out some of the food they had brought: canned fruit and vegetables, potatoes, and a lard can of bacon. When they reached Albuquerque, New Mexico, they stayed in a cabin and everyone took a bath. **5** Flossie felt strange without a home, but at least they were clean.

Across New Mexico and Arizona, they passed other Okies, farm families packed into old cars, heading for a place where they hoped "everything would be all right again." Flossie and James worried when they saw cars stranded along the way. As they neared California, it happened to them—the car broke down in the middle of nowhere. Standing under the high July sun, Flossie thought, "We're out of water, and we aren't going to make it." And then, like a miracle, she saw a boy on a bicycle riding down Route 66 on his way from Kentucky to California. He stopped, shared his water, and helped fix the car. **6** "I'm glad to see there's still some decent folks left in this world," Flossie told him gratefully.

Ahead lay the hardest driving of all, crossing the Mojave Desert. By the time they crossed the Colorado River into California, Flossie had gotten sick. 'You won't make it if you try the desert run in the heat,' a filling station attendant warned. So the Haggards camped outside Needles that day and crossed the Mojave in the cool of night. **7**

In less than a week, they had traveled from the dusty plains of Oklahoma to the green fields of the San Joaquin Valley. **8** "The good Lord was with us," Flossie said when she thought about the trip. But now the Haggards found themselves in another world of hardship. Hundreds of thousands of Okies had flooded California, looking for work. The Haggards saw family and friends living in cardboard shacks, moving from field to field, following the ripening crops. Luckily, Flossie and James were able to find work milking 40 cows a day. When September came, they moved to town so that the children could go to school. James got a job working for the Santa Fe Railroad at 40 cents an hour, and he converted an old refrigerator train car into a home. **9** With hard work and faith, Flossie and James made a new life for their family.

OKIE FACTS

■ *Okies like the Haggards came from other states as well as Oklahoma: Arkansas, Texas, Kansas, Colorado, New Mexico. Between 300,000 and 400,000 farmers lost their farms and went to California.*

■ *Drought was only one hardship for western farmers in the 1930s. The Great Depression caused an economic crisis all over the United States. In addition, small farmers like the Haggards often could not compete with corporate owners of larger and more mechanized farms.*

Saved...

1939

The Red Cross worker smiled as she handed Israel Veleris a bottle of milk. But the six-year-old boy, called Isi, heard the roar of the German bombers flying over the Brussels train station. **1** Isi clutched his mother's hand as his father tried to keep the family together in the crush of frightened people. It seemed as though the whole Jewish community of Brussels was fleeing the Nazi army that had just invaded Belgium. 'The Nazis took over Germany,' Isi's parents explained, 'and now they want to conquer the rest of Europe. They are evil, Isi. They hate us just because we are Jewish, and they will try to hurt us.'

And so Isi's exodus began. In Paris **2** the family soon decided that a country village **3** would be safer as war swept across Europe. For Isi this was a golden time. Too young to understand the true dangers, he played in the fields, went to school, and helped the village baker make his bread. Then trouble came like a dark cloud's shadow. Isi's father died. In the summer of 1940 the Nazis invaded France. And one day the French police began to arrest all of the Jews in the village. Isi and his mother hid in a barn **4** but were soon caught and sent by truck **5** to Aulus les Bains, a resort town near the Spanish border.

There they were herded together with almost 700 other Jews in the town's grand hotels. **6** Isi knew there was danger in the air. German soldiers guarded the road, and there was no way out.

But he was a child still, with a child's pleasures. While his mother worked at the grandest hotel of all, the Majestic, Isi helped the town blacksmith. He loved to pump the bellows and to hear the music of the hammer as it struck the anvil. The blacksmith was kind to the little boy in short pants, and Isi never forgot him.

By 1942, Isi's pleasure would disappear. Early one morning his mother shook him awake. 'The police are rounding up Jews,' she told Isi. While some Jews fled toward Spain, **7** Isi and his mother crept into a hiding place just outside of town. 'It will be safer for us to hide now,' she said. Days passed, and still Isi heard the footsteps outside their secret place. Soon, their food and water were gone. It seemed that the police were gone, too, so Isi's mother sent him for help. 'Sneak into the kitchen of the Majestic,' she told her son. 'The cooks are our friends, and they will give us food.'

Isi slipped quietly into the hotel. But before he could catch his breath, the terrified boy was grabbed by a police guard. In an instant Isi faced the commandant, the chief of police. 'Where have you been hiding, boy?' he demanded, as the guards slapped Isi. **8** Moments later, Isi's mother was dragged in by another guard. "Get rid of this garbage," the commandant sneered, as the guards shoved the boy and his mother onto a bus. **9** They drove them to the Camp du Vernet. **10** Its wooden barracks and barbed-wire fences enclosed hundreds of Jews and other "undesirables" rounded up by the French police.

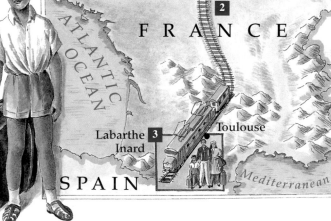

Isi and his mother knew that whatever happened next would not be good. Every day trains took away some prisoners and brought others. When 45 boys were dragged in together one day, Isi's mother discovered that they had been captured from the Swiss Red Cross in a nearby castle. When the director of the castle demanded and got the boys' return, Isi's mother knew what she had to do. Somehow, she got word to the castle: "Come quickly. Another boy awaits you." Two days later, a man arrived from the castle, insisting that Isi be turned over to him. Because it was the Swiss Red Cross, the commandant of the camp agreed. Sobbing, Isi's mother embraced her son for the last time. **11** Isi left for the castle, **12** not realizing that he would never see his mother again. The next morning, she was sent to the death camp at Auschwitz.

Isi's mother had saved her son. For the rest of the war, Isi was protected, first at the castle and then in a convent. Drawing water from the village well one day, Isi looked up into the sky to see an American soldier float down and land in the village square. **13** It was 1944, and the war in France was over. Within a few years, Isi would find himself in America. Like thousands of other Jewish children who had lost their families, their homes, and almost their lives, Isi started all over again.

ISI VELERIS FACTS

■ *Isi's mother was one of six million Jewish men, women, and children who died in Nazi concentration camps during World War II.*

■ *Today, Isi Veleris is a photographer. After many years in the United States, he lives again in France.*

"Walk Together, Children"

1965

"Walk together, children, and don't you get weary, . . . and America will be a new America," Martin Luther King, Jr., urged the crowd outside Brown Chapel in Selma, Alabama. **1** Standing in her pink jeans in the hot noon sun, young Lynda Blackmon **2** thought about the first time she had heard Dr. King speak, a year before when she was only 13 years old. "I knew that I wanted to do what he was talking about," she remembered, "and he was talking about freedom and the right to vote."

Now, as if to gather strength, 3,000 voices filled the air, singing "We Shall Overcome." Dr. King in the lead, they walked through the streets of Selma on their way to the state capitol in Montgomery, 50 miles away. An army of believers, black and white, they came from Selma and all around the nation. They marched to protest injustice, the injustice of laws and customs that made it almost impossible for black people to vote in towns like Selma.

Leaving town, the marchers crossed the Edmund Pettus Bridge. **3** Soldiers with bayoneted rifles lined the bridge to protect the marchers from angry whites. A few weeks earlier, on "Bloody Sunday," Sheriff Jim Clark's men had stopped marchers there with whips, tear gas, and beatings—Lynda had 18 stitches to prove it. Now, as helicopters circled overhead, she was more determined than ever to protest.

The marchers walked just seven miles the first day, to big tents set up in a field. **4** That night, all but 300 of the marchers boarded buses to return to town. **5** The federal judge who gave them a permit said that only 300 could march the 22 miles of narrow road through Big Swamp.

The next day, her fifteenth birthday, Lynda was terrified. Facing her tent were armed troopers like those who had beaten her so terribly on

Selma

Casey

DALLAS COUNTY

Bloody Sunday. **6** The judge had told those same men that they must protect the marchers now. Certain that she was going to die right then and there, Lynda was too frightened to move. While the others waited for her, marcher Jim Letherer promised Lynda that he would protect her, even die for her. When Lynda thought about Jim's courage in making the march on crutches, with only one leg, she knew that she could go on.

All Monday they walked along Highway 80 through the swamp. **7** Lynda strode side by side with "Marching Lilly" Brown from Birmingham. Teenaged Leroy Moton from Selma carried an American flag. And Nannie Leah Washburn from Atlanta helped her deaf and blind son, Joe. Helicopters hovered overhead while soldiers checked for possible snipers.

They stayed that night on another farm, eating hot food brought out from a church. **8** The next morning in the rain, they saw signs saying "Yankee Trash Go Home!" One passing driver mocked the marchers, but his wife tried to stop him. "They're tired and they're weary. I don't think it's funny," she said. The rain turned their stopping place into a sea of mud, **9** but Lynda didn't care. She knew where she was going and why.

Wednesday morning as the marchers left Big Swamp, soldiers checked the road and bridges for dynamite and bombs (they had found both just a few days before). Where the road widened, thousands of people swelled the march. **10** At the last campsite, St. Jude's Catholic Center on the outskirts of Montgomery, Lynda and her girlfriends from Selma watched the singers and movie stars who had come to celebrate the march. **11**

The next morning 25,000 people marched through Montgomery to the capitol building. **12** Alabama's governor, George Wallace, was not there to greet them. He stayed in his office, peeking out through the blinds. But Martin Luther King stood on the steps of the capitol and addressed the marchers. The road to getting the vote would not be smooth, he told them. "We are still in for a season of suffering," he said. "However difficult the moment, it will not be long, because truth crushed to the earth will rise again. How long? Not long." As the crowd shouted back, Dr. King continued. "How long? Not long, because no lie can live forever." Lynda Blackmon went home to Selma that night, exhausted, thrilled, and deeply proud. She believed that she had "helped to rewrite history." And she was right.

SELMA FACTS

■ *With pressure from President Lyndon Johnson, Congress passed the Voting Rights Act in July 1965. It was, Johnson said, "one of the most monumental laws in the entire history of American freedom."*

■ *Before the march only a few hundred black voters were registered in Selma. A year later, after the Voting Rights Act was signed into law, there were more than 9,000.*

Montgomery

YANKEE TRASH GO HOME

MONTGOMERY COUNTY

LOWNDES COUNTY

La Peregrinación

1966

"*Vamos a hacer una peregrinación,*" César Chávez said. "Let's make a pilgrimage." Chávez, a small Mexican American man with a shy smile, looked at the farm workers meeting with him. These were the leaders of the National Farm Workers Association. For six months, the tiny union had joined the workers striking against the grape growers around Delano, California. Workers striking for better wages and safer working conditions—this was something new. And now César Chávez was planning something else the farm workers had never done before. They would march from Delano to Sacramento, the state capital, to present their demands to the governor.

A march is "a powerful weapon," Chávez said. The farm workers needed powerful weapons in their fight against the rich growers. For generations they had struggled to survive under grueling conditions. Now, on March 17, hope and excitement were in the air. As the *peregrinación* began, 20-year-old marcher Angie Hernandez thought it looked like a big party. César Chávez was at the head of the crowd. After a few blocks, the marchers stopped short. Thirty policemen barred the way. **1** The marchers had no parade permit, the police chief said. "We'll stay here if it takes a year, but we're going to march right through the city," Chávez answered. For three hours, no one moved. Finally, grudgingly, the police moved aside.

The 68 marchers began their long walk, single file, up Highway 99. Flags waved in the sunshine as cars and big trucks roared by. And always there was the banner of the Virgin of Guadalupe, the patron saint of Mexico. She would bring them justice, the farm workers said.

Soon, César Chávez could hardly walk. "I was so busy, I didn't have time to get ready," he explained, pointing to his worn-out shoes. Leaning on Angie Hernandez's shoulder, Chávez hobbled along. **2** That first day, they walked 21 miles. Some, Angie could see, had blood oozing from their shoes. One marcher was sent home, a seven-year-old boy who had skipped school to be a pilgrim with the others.

All along the way supporters called out to the marchers, and sometimes they joined them. At each stop, townspeople opened their homes to the weary travelers. One day a family even served them cold drinks from a silver punch bowl. **3** Every night, when the marchers gathered together after the long day, Luis Valdez put on a performance of his *Teatro Campesino*, the Farm Workers Theater. **4**

When the *peregrinación* reached Modesto, other union workers came out to cheer the marchers on. **5** That night they celebrated the birthday of their beloved César Chávez. **6** A few days later, Chávez heard incredible news. A grower wanted to make peace with the union—the first time a company agreed to give the union power to make changes for the farm workers. It was a chance that Chávez could not turn down. On April 6, at one o'clock in the morning, a car raced him to Beverly Hills, **7** where he signed the contract. And then César Chávez went back to his pilgrimage.

As the march neared Sacramento, more and more supporters wanted to join the pilgrimage. But some were stopped by the growers. In one sugar beet field, the grower landed in a plane to prevent his workers from leaving. **8** Finally, on Easter Sunday morning, the marchers crossed the bridge into Sacramento. **9** By the time they reached the steps of the capitol, the crowd had grown to 10,000 people. The governor was not there to greet them, but the farm workers didn't mind. "We wanted the people there," César Chávez said. "It is well to remember there must be courage," he told them, "but also that in victory there must be humility." It was the end of the *peregrinación,* but just the beginning of the long work ahead.

FARM WORKER FACTS

■ *The marchers walked about 350 miles in 25 days, at a pace of about three and a half miles an hour. They stopped in 53 towns along the way.*

■ *The National Farm Workers Association—now the United Farm Workers of America—was the first union organized by farm workers themselves.*

■ *More than 40 people—the originales—walked every step of* la peregrinación. *Angie Hernandez was one of them.*

Sacramento

BEVERLY HILLS

Stockton

San Francisco

N

0   30   60
Miles

Modesto

Merced

Madera

Fresno

Visalia

Porterville

Delano

PACIFIC OCEAN

VIVA LA CAUSA

VIVA LA HUELGA

PEREGRI PENITEN REVOLUCI

NFWA

Losing China

1966

"No," Nien Cheng cried out, trying to stop the Red Guard from smashing the 300-year-old porcelain cup. "No one in this world can make another wine cup like this again." But the angry Red Guards paid no attention when they looted her beautiful home. **1** "The purpose of the Great Proletarian Cultural Revolution is to destroy the old culture," they shouted, to get rid of the "Four Olds": old thinking, old habits, old customs, old culture. The Red Guard was like an army run wild through the streets of Shanghai. They wanted to rid China of everything they thought was untrue to the beliefs of Chairman Mao Zedong, China's communist leader.

That night, in the ruins of their home, Nien Cheng comforted her daughter, Meiping. "When the Cultural Revolution is over, we will make a new home," she told her. "We will weather the storm together," Meiping replied. But this was not to be.

A few weeks later, on September 27, the Red Guards came again. This time, they took Nien Cheng away. A large crowd joined the Red Guards

Red Guard demonstration

Red Guard activity **3**

4

to accuse Nien Cheng of crimes against her country. **2** She was too rich, they said. She had worked for Shell Oil, a foreign company, and spied for foreign governments, they said. She must confess her crimes, they told her. When she denied committing crimes, the Red Guards handcuffed her and took her to prison. As they drove through the streets, Nien Cheng saw the smoke of burning books **3** and heard accusations being shouted at others. The Red Guard was terrorizing the city. **4**

At the Number 1 Detention House, **5** Nien Cheng was forced into a small, damp, dirty cell. From now on, she was told, she would be known only as Number 1806. As Nien Cheng looked around, her heart sank. Her only link to the outside was the tiny barred window. As those first days passed, she dreamed that her spirit "would escape through the window to freedom." But there was no freedom in the Number 1 Detention House.

Soon after she arrived, Nien Cheng was taken from her cell to be questioned. "Those who have made mistakes or committed crimes are making confessions," she was told sternly. "The purpose of this interrogation is to help you change your way of thinking." But Nien Cheng refused to lie. "I don't know how to confess to something that did not happen," she said. Over and over, year after year, Nien Cheng was brought from her cell to be questioned. Over and over, she defied her accusers. She could not,

No. 1 Detention House

she would not, confess to crimes she did not commit. She had tried to do the best for her country, and she would not lie.

Nien Cheng was allowed to read only four books, all written by Chairman Mao. One day as she sat reading, she saw a tiny spider spinning its web in the barred window. **6** Time passed, and she watched the spider make new webs when the old were torn and find protection from the cold as winter came. If the spider could go on fighting to survive, Nien Cheng thought, so could she.

Six and a half years passed. All this time, cold and hungry, Nien Cheng worried about her daughter. She knew that other prisoners sometimes received packages of clothing from their family. Why were there no packages from Meiping?

On a March day in 1973, Nien Cheng was taken to the interrogation room once again. It will be the same as always, she thought. But this day, the interrogators told her that she was being freed from prison. In six and a half years, China had changed. After U.S. president Richard Nixon had visited China in February, Chairman Mao wanted a new relationship with the United States. Prisoners with connections to the West, like Nien Cheng, were being released. Nien Cheng wanted to be declared innocent, the victim of a terrible mistake. But there was no apology.

Finally, Nien Cheng was free. But her worst fear turned out to be true. Meiping was dead, killed by the revolutionaries just a year after Nien Cheng had been sent to prison. As Nien Cheng tried to make a new life in this different world, the wounds of the Cultural Revolution were everywhere. She felt neither trusted nor trusting, watched everywhere she went. **7** Finally, she decided that she must leave China.

On September 20, 1980, Nien Cheng stood on the deck of a ship as it sailed from Shanghai. **8** She had never felt so sad. "It was a break so final that it was shattering," she later recalled. But in the United States she found a "great nation of open spaces and warm-hearted people." Like the little spider, Nien Cheng made a new place in the world.

NIEN CHENG FACTS

■ *Today Nien Cheng lives in Washington, D.C. She told the story of her imprisonment in her best-selling book* Life and Death in Shanghai.

■ *The Cultural Revolution lasted from 1966 until about 1976, when Mao Zedong died.*

"Welcome to America"

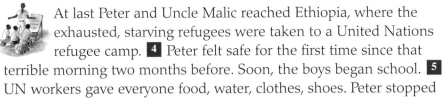

Paguere

1988

As the sun rose over the Sudan in central Africa, the air exploded with gunshots and screams. Terrified, six-year-old Peter Malual leaped from his bed and raced outside. As he looked wildly for his parents and his brothers and sisters, Peter saw his father fall to the ground, shot dead. 'Quick, run,' he heard others cry. Peter ran as fast as he could. **1**

In the bush—grassy wooded land outside the village—Peter joined hundreds of frightened villagers. But his mother, his sisters, his brothers, were not there. Sobbing, Peter felt an arm around his shoulders. It was his Uncle Malic. Together, they listened to the elders, the village leaders. 'We must leave now. It is no longer safe,' the men said. The civil war that had torn apart the Sudan for five years had reached Peter's village.

Peter, Malic, and the others began to walk toward safety in Ethiopia. They had no food, no water, and, because they had been in bed, no shoes. Peter's feet hurt and his stomach hurt, but most of all, his heart hurt. The boy cried and cried as he walked.

Across the Nile, **2** Peter saw thousands more refugees from the war. Many, like Peter, were boys who had lost their parents. For two months they moved like a slow tide through dangerous lands. **3** Along the way, long-time tribal enemies attacked the refugees with guns and spears. At night, Peter lay close to Uncle Malic and listened to the calls of nearby lions and hyenas—animals that would kill boys too weak to walk with the others.

At last Peter and Uncle Malic reached Ethiopia, where the exhausted, starving refugees were taken to a United Nations refugee camp. **4** Peter felt safe for the first time since that terrible morning two months before. Soon, the boys began school. **5** UN workers gave everyone food, water, clothes, shoes. Peter stopped crying then. "It is me now who will make things to be in my future," he realized. "If I continue to cry, maybe I will make nothing."

Then, in May 1991, when Peter was nine years old, everything changed—again. Civil war was now tearing apart Ethiopia. Once again, Peter and Uncle Malic ran for their lives. The refugees wandered for weeks, but their only choice was to return to the Sudan. When they reached the Gilo River, they were part of a huge flood of 20,000 refugees.

Crossing the river was a nightmare beyond imagining. Pursued by rebel soldiers, boys flung themselves into the rushing water. **6** Peter heard screams as crocodiles grabbed some. Most, like Peter, could not swim, but a few boys managed to string ropes across the water. Uncle Malic helped Peter grab on to a rope. As Peter pulled himself to safety on the other side, he heard the shots that killed his uncle. It was a sound that Peter Malual will never forget.

Heartsick, Peter pushed on with the 12,000 who had survived the crossing. **7** After two weeks, they reached a Red Cross camp in the Sudan. **8** When it was too dangerous to stay any longer, the Red Cross helped the refugees move to the UN camp at Kakuma in Kenya. **9** Peter would stay at Kakuma for nine years. He would grow up there, always wondering whether he would have to flee from this place too. All the while, Peter was going to school. "Because your parents are dead and cannot

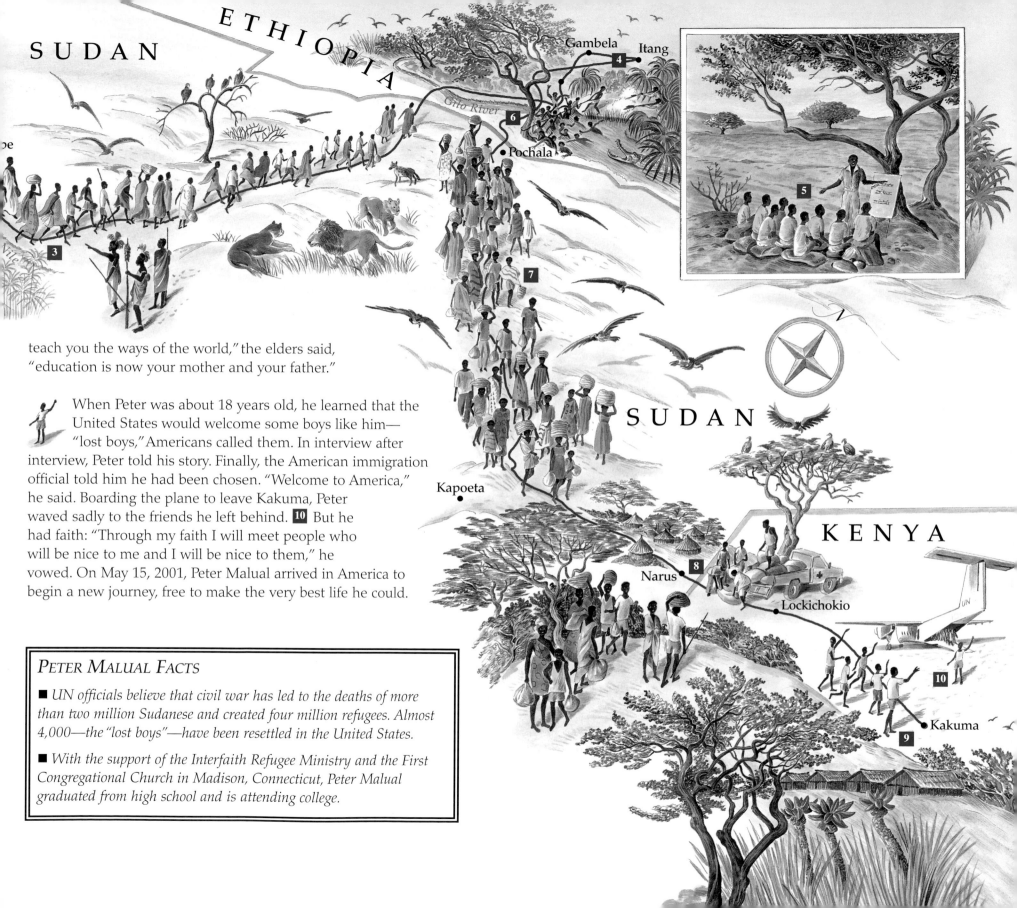

SUDAN

ETHIOPIA

Gambela   Itang

4

Gilo River

6

Pochala

3

5

7

SUDAN

N

teach you the ways of the world," the elders said, "education is now your mother and your father."

When Peter was about 18 years old, he learned that the United States would welcome some boys like him—"lost boys," Americans called them. In interview after interview, Peter told his story. Finally, the American immigration official told him he had been chosen. "Welcome to America," he said. Boarding the plane to leave Kakuma, Peter waved sadly to the friends he left behind. **10** But he had faith: "Through my faith I will meet people who will be nice to me and I will be nice to them," he vowed. On May 15, 2001, Peter Malual arrived in America to begin a new journey, free to make the very best life he could.

Kapoeta

KENYA

Narus   **8**

Lockichokio

10

PETER MALUAL FACTS

■ *UN officials believe that civil war has led to the deaths of more than two million Sudanese and created four million refugees. Almost 4,000—the "lost boys"—have been resettled in the United States.*

■ *With the support of the Interfaith Refugee Ministry and the First Congregational Church in Madison, Connecticut, Peter Malual graduated from high school and is attending college.*

Kakuma

9

Acknowledgments

Once again we have had the privilege of partnership—authors, illustrator, designer, editors. Like its predecessors *Journeys in Time* and *Places in Time*, this book could not have been created without that collaboration.

The artist Rodica Prato worked her magic to create the illustrations in exquisite detail. We thank her for being our partner and our friend.

The designer Kevin Ullrich made our ideas work on the page. His talent, friendship, and patience were invaluable now as before.

Our first editor, Amy Flynn, made this series happen in the beginning, and we thank her for her faith in us and in our dream. Emily Linsay was a gift for which we will be eternally grateful. And Eleni Beja has guided us to the end of this journey with marvelous care and skill.

As before, we have relied on the expertise and generosity of historians, librarians, archivists, and curators around the country. In addition to those listed here, we continue to be grateful to the generations of historians whose wisdom we have tapped and to the libraries where we found it (especially to the Bobst Library at New York University, the New York Public Library, and the New York Society Library).

Susan Buckley
Elspeth Leacock

Notes

Every journey and every person in this book is real. We found the stories in many places—we read them in books, we talked with historians, and sometimes we were lucky enough to interview the travelers themselves.

Through our research we found out where and how the journeys were made. And sometimes we know exactly what people said along the way. Then we have used regular quotation marks for dialogue. In other cases, we have a good idea about what people said but we do not have solid historical evidence. For this dialogue we have used single quotation marks.

To Providence

Thanks to Dr. Patricia E. Rubertone, associate professor of anthropology, Brown University; and the staff of the Pequot Museum.

Le Grand Dérangement

We were told the story of Elizabeth Brasseux by her great-great-great-great-great-great-grandson, Carl Brasseaux, who hopes that "the lessons learned from this episode of ethnic cleansing will not be lost on the next generation." Thanks to Dr. Carl Brasseaux, professor of history and assistant director, Center for Louisiana Studies, University of Louisiana at Lafayette; and Grand Pré National Historic Site, Grand Pré, Nova Scotia, Canada.

On the Forbidden Path

Almost all of the detail in this story comes from primary sources, including the journals of Christian Frederick Post and John Hays, collected in *Journey on the Forbidden Path*, edited by Robert S. Grumet. Thanks to Dr. Robert S. Grumet and Dr. Scott Stephenson.

Soldier in Disguise

Colonial spelling was not as precise as ours is. Historians differ on whether the correct spelling of Deborah's name is Samson or Sampson, and Robert Shurtliff's name was spelled several different ways. Thanks to Robert M. S. McDonald, assistant professor of history, U.S. Military Academy, West Point; the historian Dr. Carol Berkin; and Gaye Wilson, International Center for Jefferson Studies at Monticello.

Called by the Voice of America

Among the many superb references on Washington's inaugural journey, our favorite—and the most useful — was Dr. Frank Monaghan's *Notes on the Inaugural Journey and the Inaugural Ceremonies of George Washington as First President of the United States*, prepared for a reenactment at the New York World's Fair in 1939. Thanks to the Washington reenactor William Sommerfield of the American Historical Theater, Philadelphia; and Mary V. Thompson, research specialist, Mount Vernon Ladies' Association.

Buying Freedom

We discovered this remarkable story at the New York Public Library's Schomberg Center for Research in Black Culture in *Free Frank: A Black Pioneer on the Antebellum Frontier* (University Press of Kentucky, 1983) by Juliet E. K. Walker, Frank McWhorter's great-great-granddaughter. Thanks to Charles L. Blockson, Afro-American Collection, Temple University; and Jerry Raisor, historian, Fort Boonesborough.

"Give Us Free!"
Thanks to Carl Francis, *Amistad* scholar; and Charles L. Blockson, Afro-American Collection, Temple University.

A Thousand Miles for Freedom
William Craft told the story of his and Ellen Craft's escape in *Running a Thousand Miles for Freedom,* first published in London in 1860. Thanks to Charles L. Blockson, Afro-American Collection, Temple University.

Walking to Zion
We first read Peter McBride's firsthand account in *I Walked to Zion: True Stories of Young Pioneers on the Mormon Trail* by Susan A. Madsen (Deseret Book Company, 1994). Thanks to Craig Fuller, Utah State Historical Society.

"For Honor, Duty, and Liberty"
Henry Gooding's story is based on the letters that he wrote home to the *New Bedford Mercury* newspaper, collected in *On the Altar of Freedom: A Black Soldier's Civil War Letters from the Front,* edited by Virginia M. Adams (University of Massachusetts Press, 1991). Thanks to Charles L. Blockson, Afro-American Collection, Temple University; and Robert M. S. McDonald, assistant professor of history, U.S. Military Academy, West Point.

Gold Mountain
Ah Goong's story was told by his granddaughter, Maxine Hong Kingston, in her book *China Men* (Random House, 1980). Thanks to Kyle Williams Wyatt, historian/curator, California State Railroad Museum; and Lila Perl.

Flight of the Nez Perce
The quotes from Wetatonmi come from an oral history that she gave after the flight. Thanks to Darlene Christiansen, Timothy Fisher, and John James at Big Hole National Battlefield; Robert Applegate, Nez Perce National Historic Park; and Josiah Pinkham, Cultural Resources Department of the Nez Perce.

The Promised Land
Mary Antin told her story in her book *The Promised Land,* first published in 1912. Thanks to Erica Blankstein, project archivist, Yivo Institute of Jewish Research.

Going North
Mildred Arnold told her story to Giles Wright in an oral history recording. Thanks to Dr. Giles R. Wright, director, Afro-American History Program, New Jersey Historical Commission; and Charles L. Blockson, Afro-American Collection, Temple University.

The Road to California
We first found the Haggard family story in "Route 66" by Thomas Pew, *American Heritage* magazine, August 1977. Additional details come from Merle Haggard's memoir *My House of Memories* (Cliff Street Books, 1999).

Saved . . .
Isi Veleris shared with us, in an interview, the harrowing story of his childhood. Thanks to Isi Veleris and Rodica Prato.

"Walk Together, Children"
Lynda Blackmon told us her story of the Selma march in an interview. Thanks to Lynda Blackmon; Edmund Pettus Bridge National Voting Rights Museum and Institute; and Charles L. Blockson, Afro-American Collection, Temple University.

La Peregrinación
In addition to the valuable accounts found in the many books written about César Chávez and *la peregrinación,* we relied on *El Malcriado: The Voice of the Farm Worker,* the newspaper published by the Farm Worker Press. Thanks to Julie Rodriguez, Cesar E. Chavez Foundation; and Kathy Schmelling, Reuther Library, Wayne State University.

Losing China
Nien Cheng told her story in her book *Life and Death in Shanghai* (Grove Press, 1986) and in conversations with us. Thanks to Nien Cheng.

"Welcome to America"
Peter Malual told us his story in an interview—"so others will understand what I have faced and what is going on in my country," he said. Thanks to Peter Malual; Carol Brown and Sharon Mackwell of the Interfaith Refugee Ministry; Joe Roberson of the Church World Service; and Reverend Charles Freeland.

Index